KIDS, COCKTAILS, & CONUNDRUMS

PARENTING FROM BIRTH TO ADULTHOOD, PLUS THE DRINK RECIPES I USED TO SURVIVE THE JOURNEY!

NICOLE BILLS

DEDICATION

Parents—For my life, love, faith, and knowledge; you have my gratitude, love, and respect.

Friends—You know who you are. You who've long toiled with me. You who have celebrated "the wins" with me. Who've listened, assuaged, and lamented with me over my fears, tears, and misery. The ones who have helped me pour over the writing of this book. You. I'd be lost without y'all's friendships. There are not enough words in the English language to properly describe my love for each of you.

Children—Without you I would never be called a mother—the title that brings my greatest joy in life. — Katharine, I love you until Africa and China meet. Austin, I love you to the ends of the ever-expanding universe.

Husband—You are, as always, the reason I get anything done and the reason I am able to be brave in life. I olive juice you forever and ever.

CONTENTS

THE TOO OBVIOUS DISCLAIMER

I've done some great parenting and have also royally messed up. I've researched the rights and wrongs of successful parenting, and now I'm writing about it. Does that make me an expert? Heck yes! Does that make me a professional? Nope. Have questions? Seek out a professional—it's just a good idea. And don't drink and parent—that's never a good idea. If you need help, seek help. This book was written with the intent to make you laugh and feel less alone.

This page has been left blank for your planning or notes

CHAPTER 1: AN INTRODUCTION OF SORTS

"Everybody knows how to raise children except the people who have them." -Dadonymous

Hi. So, at this point, you will have noticed I have skipped the usual parts of the book we all tend to skip. I was just too excited and wanted to jump right in with you. As I haven't written a book that you have to read in sequential order of chapters, I take moments like these at the beginning of each chapter to outline what I write about making it easier for you and me to find things quickly, because honestly, who has the time…

- Who the feck is Nicole?
- What is the point?
- What is a Carrytail?
- This book and the stuff you should know

I am truly grateful that you have picked up this book during your busy life and are committed to giving it a go. I hope that you find at least one nugget of wisdom, a ton of laughs (even if they are at my expense), and wonderful drink recipes to enjoy with yourself, your kids, friends, and family.

MY NAME IS NICOLE

I am a wife to my best friend from high school and a mother of two teens who have taught me everything I know about forgiveness and counting to ten (sometimes 10 million) for patience. I love any excuse to gather with friends and family for an evening of shenanigans, or for a weekend of fancy cocktails, good times and fellowship.

With my amazing husband by my side, I have struggled to graduate from university studying education and psychology, raise and educate our two kids while traveling, and for kicks run a couple of businesses while aspiring to write really great sh*t.

My parenthood has been anything but fancy. It has been one of the most difficult - often poop covered - jobs I have ever done. I know there are parents out there who have it all together and look great while doing it. They somehow have managed to raise darlings, host the perfect parties, and keep not just their sanity but also their figure.

I am not them.

I think they are great, but I am also very ok with not being a part of that club. I do not have it all and I never seem to have enough time in the day to rule the world, train the circus I am raising, or get out of my messy bun and yoga pants that I may or may not have slept in for the last two days.

I have found through 20+ years of parenting that beer and wine, though easy enough to pour, are not always enough for some of the messed-up hurdles I have had to face while raising two suck-the-life-out-of-me-monsters-who-are-equally-beautiful-gifts-that-deliver-purpose-and-joy-to-my-otherwise-mundane-existence.

Enter my fancy libations for surviving parenthood.

Whether they have alcohol in them or not (aka Carrytails – I explain this in a little bit), we parents need a moment of fancy. We need a diversion that offers us a moment of bliss while arguing with tinier versions of ourselves about how to wipe up spills, not to pee on the neighbor's dog…again, the merits of driving responsibly, and to PLEASE-FOR-THE-LOVE-OF-ALL-THAT-IS-HOLY put on longer pants before we go visit grandma!

Yes, I do realize that the "industry" has marketed to the growing love of cocktails and has created a vast array of premade mixes and pre-flavored liquor, waters, and kombuchas. Some are great, most are not, some days you just need it easy and, on those days, it is fine to give those a try. For me, I like to know and control how much sugar and flavor is in each drink and that it is going to match my expectations. I can testify that after the 5+ years of putting this book together, fresh recipes always win over the premade ones.

PONTIFICATION

I wanted a platform to encourage my fellow comrades in the good fight of raising children during this modern era. I have seen too many of us become our own greatest enemy, tearing each other down with well-placed passive aggressive comments.

The thing that makes parenting hard, aside from the emotions, self-doubt, social media versions of perfection and long hours is that every human is completely different and yet alike at the same time. What works for one, won't work for another. We need to know and tell each other daily that we are already enough. We are, for better or worse, exactly who our kids need us to be. It is our jagged human edges that create the truth-texture needed for others to grasp what it is they need to know or learn about themselves.

Let's get real and comfortable with not really being sure if we are doing it right. Let's pick each other up and encourage one another to keep trying. Then mix a drink, laugh at ourselves and bond over the equal amounts of pain and joy that parenting brings.

In this little book, you now hold in your hands, I have compiled the dark humor of parenting, my personal highs and lows, along with some things that I have seen work and are worth trying. Subsequently, I also am giving you some doozies that I definitely think we should all collectively agree to not do. I have ordered this book in two-year increments up to the age of 21 before I get into being a parent of a full-grown adult.

WHY THE ORDER OF DRINKS?

I have paired excellent drink recipes in ascending order of alcohol content. The idea was that the younger the child, the less alcohol was needed to function properly. Conversely, the older the kid, the more that might be needed for some of the turmoil that kids can put you through.

The names of the drinks vary. Some of them I have kept the most common name by which they are known. Others are recipes that I have come up with, named for either the place they were conceived or for the element that makes them stands out.

COCKTAILS & CARRYTAILS

Cocktails are obvious when you order them at the bar, you are expecting alcohol in a mixture of sorts. In the early 1800's "professor" Jerry Thomas gave us one of the first "bittered sling" books about all the variant ways to mix stimulating liquors with sugar, water, and bitters. The genesis story of the name is obscured by time in history, but it makes sense to me that it might have come from NOLA (New Orleans, Louisiana), where bartenders used a "coquetel" aka eggcup to serve up the invention; thus, born the American pronunciation of cocktail.

What I want to know though, is who let "mocktail" or "virgin" catch on? I am not sure what it is supposed to evoke, am I being mocked for ordering it? Or am I carelessly mentioning whether I have come to know someone intimately between the sheets – or not, all within one drink order? Any which way it doesn't sit right with me.

When writing this book, I knew I was never going to use those words outside of the above paragraph. I looked up synonyms for the "M-word" and do you know what is the one and only phrase generated? "Kiddie cocktail". Seriously?! As though only a child would drink one. There are all kinds of reasons and seasons not to drink alcohol that have nothing to do with being too young or legally able to drink.

It is past time to name it something more valiant, more respectable. A word that makes me feel justified not ridiculous when ordering it. My search began.

In the first year of this book's sh*tty first draft, I used "Victorian cocktails". I pigheadedly demanded all my friends to make it a thing and start saying it. No one cared for it. I was explaining it to a sweet friend, and she said, "Oh, kind of like a Baptist?" that tickled my funny bone. I thought it might stick, but with some research, it turns out Victorians (and some Baptists) drink. So, those were out.

In my research, I did, however, stumble upon the warrior, Carrie Amelia Nation.

This was a six-foot-tall hatchet carrying bada** of a woman, who fought valiantly for temperance. She lost her first husband to alcoholism and it ransacked her. I don't agree with prohibition, but I do understand loss and passion.

I fell in love with Carrie Amelia's story. She was fighting during a time when women were not valued. She was a fearless rebel who refused the status quo of her gender. She ditched her corset, picked up a hatchet and swung it at the establishment. Fight on sister!

Understanding the value of marketing, she changed her name to trademark it, Carry A. Nation. Savvy gal. This is who we should be paying homage to drinks without alcohol. I give you #carrytails - spread it.

HOW TO READ THIS BOOK

There are at least four ways to enjoy this book:
  1. Open to a random page - read and enjoy.
  2. Start at the beginning and read to the end. (Drinking responsibly).
  3. Choose an "age" that you are dealing with, mix those corresponding drinks, curl up and read.

Then there is my favorite way:

Get together with good friends, pick out a spirit, find the corresponding drink recipes and take turns opening to a favorite age, read out loud, and enjoy a few laughs while sharing your own experiences. Spending time with other parents who can relate to what you are going through is crucial to building a community. It will give you the confidence you need to forge ahead in the moments where you feel like you are shattered glass on the inside.

We, as busy parents, often forget the value of friendship. We "get along and move along" until we are depleted, and left wondering "why?". I will get into this stuff later to remind you of what you already know about fellowship but for now… how great is this book for an excuse to call up a friend?!

Pick your method, try another, share with your friends, and email me, nicole@nicolebills.com, anytime with your thoughts.

P.S. SOME HIGHLIGHTS:

Because we all do parenting differently, I wanted to share some great problem-solving strategies from parents around the world. I gave them a special showcase, and after each chapter, I've included one or two for your reading pleasure. (in some situations, the names have been changed to protect the …*ahem*… innocent)

One of my favorite things to do is to go through my mother-in-law's recipes and see all the notes she has left over the years. When I started hosting gatherings, I imitated her and wrote down dates, names, and comments with my friends and family about what they loved or hated about the recipe. It remains to be one of the things my close friends love doing when they come over. We look through my recipe books and find quotes and add funny stories to them through the years. I have intentionally left some space with each cocktail for you to write fun notes, memories, and personal taste changes that you have made with your friends.

You will notice throughout the book there are callouts. These are things of interest, where the science gets neat, or I have a good tip for you to follow.

There are multiple variations that will be noted below some of the recipes, for example how you can change the drink entirely or add/omit some of the ingredients. Some of these are in-depth and other changes are simple, but I didn't want you to miss out on anything.

At the beginning of each chapter, I have included a quote from Dadonyomous or Momonymous. These are some of the funniest statements that I have heard or read over the years. I know that all parents have felt or thought about these at one time or another, therefore, I feel they belong to all of us.

Just for fun, I have taken a photo of each main drink recipe with a fun surrounding backdrop filled with what we all typically have in our daily lives at the corresponding child-age that that chapter is named after.

(This page has been left blank for your planning or notes)

CHAPTER 2: OBSTREPEROUS AGE OF ZERO TO THE TRUCULENT TWOS

"Don't worry, you are not the first woman to throw a towel over the peed-on sheets and go back to bed."- -Momonymous

In this chapter, we will cover:

- The importance of sleep
- Why you are happy - but not really
- Finding your tribe and the rules to follow
- When and how they learn
- The meaning of tantrums

All while you are dealing with noisy babies and aggressively defiant two-year-olds. Don't worry, I have you covered with the Carrytail G.Y.A.U.A.M, Ace of Spades, and a Basil Martini (plus its Carrytail variation).

Whether it is your very first pregnancy or your 10th baby, you are in one of the most physically exhausting periods of parenthood. There is no sleep to be had and though you'll gradually get a minute more with each passing year, it's going to take until they are 25 before you get a full night's rest – just kidding… *it won't be until they are at least 30.*

I am not sure if sleep even happens at that stage. My oldest is 18 as I write this chapter. I've heard rumors from my own parents and my beloved friends that are in the 30+ kids club that it is only when they hit their mid-thirties that we get to rest.

While kissing the head of your child is the most satisfying thing you can do on this earth, parenthood will require 33.3 more work hours per week per child! If you could look at your schedule right now, where would you take those hours from? This, plus the sleep deprivation makes it an exceedingly difficult starting point in your life. Take time to reinvest and recalibrate your expectations to understand that life as you know it is going to be completely different than you thought and prepared yourself for.

You are starting to fall madly in love with this little being. You thought you knew love when you got your first pet, then you fell in love with your partner. Then, it is the first moment you connect with your child, you will be flooded with an indescribable love that seems like your heart just might break from the eruption.

Then they turn two-years-old.

By the time they are two, you will have come to learn that you can experience a range of emotions you did not know was possible for a person to go through. In a matter of seconds, you can run an emotional gamut of fear and anger. When you find yourself here, don't worry, you are not alone. We have all been through it.

Your first steps into parenthood with each individual child (yes, you are different with each one that you bring into the family) is where you will be taxed to the max of what you can do while surviving with virtually no sleep. It's weird, right? …*Here raise this little human, make life or death choices for them – with no sleep…*

HERE IS WHAT YOU DON'T KNOW

There are a few things about sleep we need to realize. It is essential for our bodies to function. We all know this intuitively. I am sure we have even all heard of those who have pushed the boundaries to the extreme and gone without sleep for days, they were certainly not the better for it. Yet, we all ignore it because we think, well that's not me. I only miss a few hours binging on tv or working late. We all think to ourselves, "I'll catch up on sleep during the weekend."

One hour of missing sleep takes away two cognitive years of function. The average human, regardless of age, needs about 8 hours of sleep. Period.

This little factoid used to stress my teen daughter out, especially during her sleepless senior year of high school. This was the year that she turned the freeing age of 18. She had to quickly learn the balance of making choices; stay out late - because she could - or meet the impending deadlines of projects that would determine graduation and final grades.

Nobody likes the idea of "period – no room for negotiation" so the idea of shift-sleeping occurs. It sounds like a great idea, have a regular sleep schedule during the week. But during the weekend we allow ourselves to stay up late and then sleep in to compensate. It seems like you are still getting the compulsory eight hours – perfect solution.

Except, sleep is not cumulative. You can't catch up.

Unfortunately, there have been numerous studies, each with similar results, for every hour of weekend shift-sleep it will cost seven points on an IQ test. Freaking. Seven. Points. (I don't think most of us have that much to spare!)

We are supposed to parent little people, keep them from dying, and teach them to be decent law-abiding citizens. All while we function as though our daily diet consists of lead paint. Which by the way, as a child born in the seventies, I am pretty sure I ate.

COMPLETELY IN LOVE AND UNHAPPY

You have an amazing life, you have a beautiful new child, you are a little tired and a lot sad. You tell yourself you shouldn't be. You explain away your feelings to your friends so that you don't seem ungrateful and depressed, but you really are having a hard time.

Guess what one culprit is? Yes, a lack of sleep. It robs your ability to recall pleasant memories and makes it easier to remember the gloomy ones. Annoying isn't it? You can't sleep ...*because hello - baby*. But you have got to sleep because otherwise, it is a downward spiral into idiocy and oblivion.

If you are here, take a deep breath and tell yourself that it is completely understandable and normal. There is nothing wrong with you, you just need some shut eye. When people give you the advice of sleeping when the baby sleeps, don't roll your eyes and think, "Yeah, like that is going to happen, that is when I can get stuff done!" I definitely used to do this. When my babies slept, I worked like crazy.

I may just be getting into my curmudgeon years, but I am tired of hearing, "You can have it all!" Looking back on my life I realized I didn't have it all. We humans can't multitask, and we parents can't have it all. I mean you can try, and you should definitely have every right to try, but ultimately, you will have to choose which thing is more important right then. Some years I chose parenting, others my work. The years that I chose parenting are where I grasped a sliver of a straw about what Einstein referred to in the Theory of Relativity. It felt like an eternity at the time when raising the little ones, now it seems so fleeting.

My advice? Take the advice. Screw ambition. Cuddle that munchkin and take a nap, you'll be smarter and happier for it.

THREE VITAL RULES TO PLAY BY

You are functioning on the lowest setting and you are learning what overwhelming love for another being feels like. Don't freak out. It is going to be ok, there are just three rules to memorize.

Rule number 1: "Parenthood equals judgment from the entire world".

No matter what you do you will get judged. Even if you do everything "right". You'll be judged for it from all walks of life. People without kids, fellow parents, your parents, even me. I'm judging you even though I don't know you from Adam. Who will be the one person to be your worst critic by far? No, surprisingly, it is not your mother! It is you.

WHAT TO DO?

Stand firm in your convictions but be flexible enough to learn from your mistakes. Yes, I realize that advice has a split-personality. Through my life, I have come to realize how grayer all life-rules become. Essentially, you've got to know what you think is right and not be afraid to do it. Don't paint yourself into a Dunning-Kruger corner, one where you think you are the omniscient-infallible-parent. Inevitably, what will happen is - you will be wrong, and everyone will be able to see where you are wrong, except for you.

Dunning-Kruger: the cognitive bias in which people mistakenly assess their ability as greater than it is. Like when you know you are totally right... but you are totally wrong.

The trick is: Be open to learning from yourself.

Every parent out there regardless of how Pinterest-y, well-read or perfect they look, have all at some point royally screwed up. In fact, right now they are probably secretly paying the therapy bills for it. When you realize you have messed up, change it. A great life mantra that I now live by is, "When you know better, do better."

Rule number 2 of early parenting is: "Hold your baby as long as you want".

Even if you are a "Sarah Cynthia Silvia Stout who would not take the garbage out", the character from Shel Silverstein's poems, or a "Sorry boss, I didn't get that presentation done because I was smelling my kids' hair" kind of person, holding your kid is one thing you will never ever regret.

I worked and went to school all through the early years of my parenting, I don't have any regrets, other than how quickly this stage of parenthood goes by. I have studied until the wee hours of the morning and given sleep-deprived presentations with my babies strapped onto my person. Those memories of my sweet babies are what keeps me sane throughout these teenage years. Snuggle, snuggle, snuggle, and repeat; it goes way too bleeping fast.

Rule number 3 of early parenting has three parts: "Find your tribe, AND ask for help, AND offer to help the members of your tribe".

Parenting is the hardest thing you will ever do in this life; I think. I am only 39.75 at the exact moment I am writing this paragraph, but from what I do know, this is it. Surround yourself with good people. Those you can trust to hold your kid while you nap, in exchange you can hold their hand while they weep.

Giving takes receiving. Give yourself to the tribe and build strong connections. Always be willing to go the extra mile for them, and they will do the same for you. And well, if they don't, then karma.

People need people; even loners need people sometimes. You get to decide how much time you spend with them. Quality is always better than quantity when it comes to relationship building. Feel free to say "no" if you need to recharge. Yet don't be afraid to say "yes" to a new adventure, even if it throws your schedule out-of-whack and you have to jump through hoops to find a sitter.

98% of your parenting gets done in the middle of these life moments and innocuous conversations with strangers and friends. How you show up in the world, and how you show up in relationships is what your "mini-me" is always watching for and they will, eventually, mimic this behavior.

I see it so plainly in my children's twilight teen years and I wish that I had known it earlier. But there is always good news. I know it now and see the changes in them now as I have made changes to my own self-improvement. Jesus, Gandhi, Mohamad, and Buddha all taught that change starts from within and that the one thing that matters most, is how we treat others. So, do that. Karma can be unpleasant when you are reaping what you've sown into this life from your children.

BABBLING AND CUTE

I've welcomed you into parenting by confirming that you'll be doing your hardest work at the most difficult level when you are not at your best and the three rules you need to play by just to get through it. But, what about your kid? What is the most important thing to know about them?

I have run an education consulting business for the last 15 years. The majority of my clients have fallen into two categories. Either kids who don't fit the mold for learning and who, for unknown reasons, despite all the resources available to them, are falling through the cracks and getting left behind. On the other hand, there are the parents who want to learn how to teach their school-age children. The last three years, I have had a ton of expectant and/or nursing mothers calling for desperate advice. They want to know what to do and how to do it when it comes to ensuring they provide their child with an optimal learning environment. At first, I was incredulous. When I was at that point in my parenting, I was consumed with thoughts about would natural childbirth kill me, or if I was putting those impossibly small socks on right …*who came up with crib shoes and what purpose do they really serve?!*…

Then I looked at the marketing aimed at expectant parents. Wow! Nowadays, you guys are bombarded with educational items that you HAVE to get to develop your baby's brain… and what kind of horrible cheapskate parent would not want to do that?...

I have come to realize that there are experts for whatever echo chamber you want to put yourself into. I tend to think that if you are the kind of parent that is asking these questions, you are probably already aware and attentive thereby giving more to your child than the majority of the world. However, I know that does little to be a salve to your worry. So, for the top two questions, I have found the top two most agreed upon solutions. If you are mastering these, you really are doing the best job that you can.

WHEN ARE BABIES READY TO LEARN?

Babies' babble isn't meaningless. Up until three months, a babies' babble is mostly fussy sounds. But at three to four months their vocal cords open and they are able to make an "O-A" sound. When you hear this, look to see what they are looking at and have a conversation with them about it. This is the best groundwork you can do. Babble equals conversation and they are ready to learn.

HOW CAN YOU BE READY TO HELP THEM?

Around six months they are able to make consonant sounds and then at nine months comes the "BA-MA" sounds that most people interpret as the beginning of word formation. Though they are ready for learning before, this is the time when most parents start to have more conversations with their little ones. "Ba? Did you say ba? Yes, that is a ball! Good job. Do you want the ball?"

Parents are right to recognize that when babbling is happening their baby is not just babbling, they are communicating, looking to you for immediate social feedback loops. The one thing to keep in mind is not to just talk about anything that comes to your mind. Talk about the things that your baby is directly looking at.

BECOME TANTRUM READY

Winter is coming. Are you ready?

One thing I wish I knew when I had kids between the ages two and four was how to code their tantrums.

When was it serious? As I mentioned earlier, at this stage you are exhausted, and tantrums can be publicly humiliating. It feels like your child is the loudest screamer ever and the world is judging your ineptness. They are, and it doesn't matter how well you handle it. Someone knows better, so don't waste your time with self-shame and doubt.

Here is the thing, the only thing that you need to concern yourself with is - are you providing the right message to your child and how much distress is okay for them to work through.

IGNORE IT

When you tell your child, "No you can't do that or can't have that" and they pitch a fit, you are better off ignoring the tantrum. Prepare yourself, these tantrums will be full of distress, they will be punctuated by anger, but it will all be over soon enough. You will feel flabbergasted as to why they suddenly hate their feet; their favorite socks that they want to wear every day are suddenly too tight; or that they don't want to eat, even though, you know they are crying because they are starving (that the toast is too toasty right now!).

Tantrums can seem nonsensical. But remember, this is not the time to get to the bottom of it. Don't ask questions. I know we all want our children to channel their inner Socrates and calmly reason, having the judgment of King Solomon when they get older, but right now they are full of emotion and anger. They are not going to be able to reason or be reasoned with. Talking can be done after they have gotten it out of their system and are ready to be consoled. Otherwise, you are just prolonging and stressing them out more by asking them to verbalize something they don't necessarily have the capacity to understand or verbally process what they are feeling at that moment in time.

Just let them be.

I mean, if it is a full restaurant, maybe go outside far enough away from the door and let them be – because that sh!t is annoying for the rest of us who have already gone through those years of parenting! I know, it seems like those who are parents should have more patience and understanding, but what you don't know yet, because you are in the midst of it, is that once you are through those battles, you will do anything to not be triggered.

STOP THE REBELLION

If you have asked them to do something specifically like, "put on your coat" or "pick up your shoes", that is not a tantrum you can avoid. The secret is to take away their autonomy – the ability to do it themselves or make their own choices. That is a trick I wish I had known when mine were little, but I take full advantage of it now with my teens.

As a toddler, you want to tell them, "Hey, you have 8 seconds to do what I asked, or I am going to help you do it". After you count (in your head – not out loud that might end up causing undue drama and anxiety in your child), then take your hands placing them over their hands with the intention of helping them do the request.

This is incredibly unpleasant for a child because you have now taken their autonomy.

The magic in this is that they would rather do as they were told as long as it means they get to remain independent. I say magic because that is what you want to encourage in your child, autonomy. It is the magic that helps them become self-sufficient, curious, successful adults.

You are never going to feel like you got it quite right; that is okay, none of us do. Don't take it personal, none of it is, even when they contract sudden hatred of you. They are in the process of learning how to be a human and you are in the process of teaching them. Remind yourself daily that your endgame is to raise a child into a healthy and successful adult who is in the pursuit of happiness. That does, however, mean that currently, you will not always have a well-behaved child.

But you can always make yourself a drink.

You are about to see your first recipes! Here are some key things I want you to know before we dive in:

EVERYTHING IS SUGGESTIVE

You have the freedom to change it up any way you want. These are just the methods and proportions that I have discovered over the last five years and, well, I think taste good. Yes, I have had my liver tested to make sure that it is still functioning. The good news is, the liver is the only organ in the body that can regenerate - I think.

Different brands are going to change the flavor profile. With these recipes, if I have an opinion on a particular spirit, I make a suggestion according to my tastes. But if you know you already have a favorite, by all means, go with that one.

WHEN BUYING SPIRITS

I always go for middle of the road - not a well, but not a top shelf. I want something that is decent to drink on its own but isn't going to break my budget, we are raising kids after all. I don't do bottom shelf - cheap stuff, because I like to pretend that I have a palate.

DOES GLASSWARE EVEN MATTER

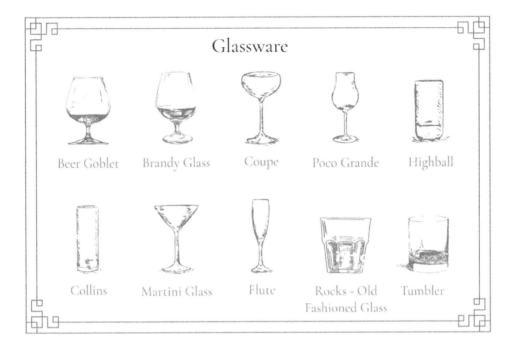

I mean, you are a busy parent, the fact that you are taking the time to read my book and mix yourself a drink for some "me time", then NO – it doesn't. I have mentioned the kinds of glasses that are typically used only for information sake, in case you were in a trivia game, or the kids have moved out and you can afford to splurge on stemware. But you use the sippy cup if you want; it's your party – and rules are made to be broken! Use what is clean (or, at least, reasonably clean) to serve yourself some decadence.

Why does anyone worry about it? The purpose of glassware is a two-fold. First, is a utilitarian matter. The glass can aid or take away from the olfactory sense of the cocktail. If it is an open mouth glass; the scent dissipates faster than if it is a narrower opening glass. The second purpose is purely ego. What glassware you are using makes you feel like you have the ego you want to present to the world. Perceptions are fueled by the glass in your hand. In the early years of cocktails, the finer and more intricate the glass meant the deeper the pockets of the person drinking it.

Three Things That Do Matter Regardless:
1. The amount that you mix may or may not fit in your cup of choice.
2. With Moscow Mules, the copper does create a chemical reaction that heightens the taste of the drink. I will let you know which mixes this is important for and which variations you can skip the science.
3. Frost whatever chalice you are using for all your cold drinks. Trust me, it tastes better. By the same token, flash the chosen vessel with hot water for whatever hot drinks you are mixing.

THAT ONE TIME IN FIFTH GRADE

Do you remember that one time in fifth grade when your English teacher was trying to get you to write an essay on "How To Do" something? My teacher gave us the assignment prompt of "teaching an alien how to make a peanut butter and jelly sandwich". Guys, I can vividly recall arguing with her about NEVER NEEDING TO KNOW HOW TO DO THIS, in the middle of class. I know, what a punk I was. If you are reading this, Miss. Sorryihavetotallyforgottenyournamebutyoutaughtatmillsapelementaryinhoustontexas… I am deeply sorry. I have absolutely had to use this said skill while writing this very book.

I have tried my best to write the steps as detailed as possible for a person that has never done it before – I had no idea how hard that was going to be. In my defense, I think I only got a "C" on that paper, and I am fully aware that that is not much of a defense. Prior to publishing, I have had testers go over the instructions and so far, they have done alright. Of course, they might have been a little tipsy after a few of the drinks.

Have fun with it! When in doubt, do your best and then feel free to blame my argumentative 5th grade-self of the past, if all doesn't turn out as we hoped.

G.Y.A.U.A.M (1 cup of Get Your A** up in the A.M.)

Carrytail | Blend | Coffee Mug | 1 large serving

I love all my children equally. Except the one that sleeps in. I love that one the most.

INGREDIENTS
4 oz. Brewed strong coffee or espresso
4 oz. Coconut milk
1 tsp. Turmeric powder
1 tbsp. Coconut oil melted
Optional sweetener of choice (stevia, sugar, agave, honey, etc.)

STEP 1
Brew hot coffee as usual.

STEP 2
Add all ingredients to a blender and blend on high until frothy. Add to your flashed mug and enjoy.

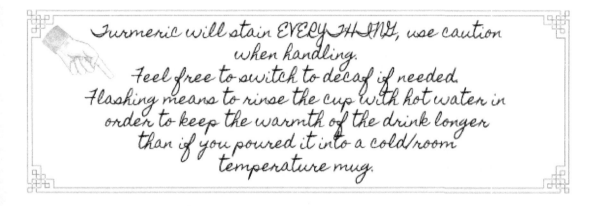

Turmeric will stain EVERYTHING, use caution when handling.
Feel free to switch to decaf if needed.
Flashing means to rinse the cup with hot water in order to keep the warmth of the drink longer than if you poured it into a cold/room temperature mug.

This page has been left blank for your planning or notes)

ACE OF SPADES
Cocktail | Shake | Martini Glass | 1 serving
Nothing tests a parent like being karate chopped in the throat by their co-sleeping 2-year-old.

INGREDIENTS
5 Ripe blackberries + 3 more for garnish
1 Small grape tomato
0.5 oz. Simple syrup
1.5 oz. Tequila blanca
0.5 oz. Lemon juice + peel
Ice

STEP 1
Pop the blackberries, tomato, and simple syrup at the bottom of your shaker and muddle with the end of a wooden spoon.

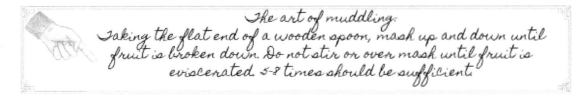

The art of muddling.
Taking the flat end of a wooden spoon, mash up and down until fruit is broken down. Do not stir or over mash until fruit is eviscerated. 5-8 times should be sufficient.

STEP 2
Pour in your tequila and shake vigorously with ice for a count of 10.

STEP 3
Strain into a frosted glass and garnish your drink with a toothpick balanced on the rim with 3 skewered blackberries a pierced lemon peel to enjoy.

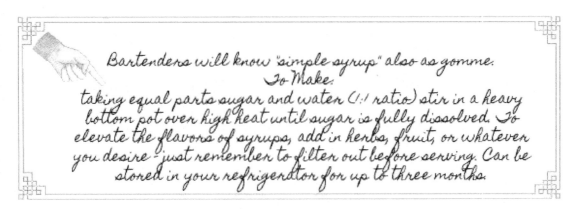

Bartenders will know "simple syrup" also as gomme.
To Make:
taking equal parts sugar and water (1:1 ratio) stir in a heavy bottom pot over high heat until sugar is fully dissolved. To elevate the flavors of syrups, add in herbs, fruit, or whatever you desire - just remember to filter out before serving. Can be stored in your refrigerator for up to three months.

This page has been left
blank for your planning
or notes

BASIL MARTINI
Cocktail | Shake | Martini Glass | 1 serving

Potty training around our house is known as Game of Thrones. We are always trying to find the one with the least amount of pee on it.

INGREDIENTS
9 basil leaves + extra for garnish
1 tsp. Simple syrup *(see pg. 30 for directions)*
0.5 oz. Lemon juice
Dash orange bitters
2 oz. Vodka
1 oz. Pineapple juice
Ice

STEP 1
Slap 7 basil leaves in between your hands.

STEP 2
With a wooden spoon handle muddle syrup, lemon juice, 7 slapped basil at the bottom of your cocktail shaker.

STEP 3
Dash in your bitters and muddle again.

STEP 4
Pour your vodka and pineapple juice into the rest of the ingredients and add 2 more basil leaves.

STEP 5
Muddle lightly again, then cover with ice and shake for a count of 10.

STEP 6
Strain into frosted glass, garnish with extra basil leaves and enjoy.

CARRYTAIL VARIATION:
Omit the vodka and in its place, use sparkling water.

Slapping the herbs will help to release the oils, providing a delicate sensation to your olfactory senses.

I am an Austin, Texas girl and therefore my favorite local sparkling water is a delicious local brand, Waterloo. Choose whichever one you like to use.

HOW OTHER PARENTS DO IT:

This Is Serious Business.

"I think the most important thing to convey to kids is that you are serious straight away. Let them know you are not budging from whatever rules you have set down for them.

I've got five kids, from tweens to 10.5-month-old twins. They all know when mamma says 'no' – she means it.

My one 10.5-month-old twin will grab onto potted plants to pull down and play in the dirt. The first time she did I said, 'Ah! Ah! – NO. That's not a good choice – don't make it.' She did it again. I flicked her hand lightly. 'No. Make a better choice.' She didn't. When she went for it again, she had a grin. I guess now it's has become a fun sadistic game for her. Maybe it is because she is my third, but I knew that I had to nip it in the bud. I flicked her culpable hand again, enough to let her know I meant business but not enough (obviously) to leave any redness. 'No.' I repeated in a low serious voice.

Now, when she does try to go for something, she will look around to see if I am around. Surprise kid, yes, I am still here. I'll say, 'No.' She, of course, pretends to have not malfeasant thoughts… but she doesn't touch it - & that's all I care about. My no means no."

-Krista, CA.

❋ My Opposing Opinion ❋

Every parent is going to feel differently about corporal punishment. Though I have been in both camps thorough my parentage and have read research to support as well as defame the use of it, as an older parent, I am not in favor of it. The more I witness other parents rely on it I have become acerbly opposed to it. Aside from sending a confusing message, especially when we tell our kids not to hit other people, this form of punitive measures is what shuts the mind-body down. Being hit, or verbally threatened with being hit sends a mass number of stress-inducing hormones raging through our bodies and that retards our mental ability to grasp and retain information.

I agree our no should mean NO. However, I think the lowering of our voice and the look of disappointment can convey this message clear enough, we just need to be careful that we do not laugh or show pleasure at those cute sassy displays at this age. I know it looks cute right now, but in a few months, you are not going to think that; instead, you will be wondering where this little monster came from.

You might be currently thinking, "Nicole, it has been a long time since you were a mother of little toddlers", and you would be correct, it has been a long time for me! But, dear reader, I currently (as of the writing of this insert) have a two and five-year-old living with me. And for the past month, I have had the pleasure of exercising this parenting muscle ALL OVER AGAIN. I still stand firm in the resolve that I am trying to convey. Don't spank or threaten to do so. That is a quick fix with serious long-term consequences.

So, why did I even include this story? I debated it with myself and with friends for a long time whether I should or not. Ultimately, I decided that these stories are of how other parents do it... I know I can trust you to judge for yourself if this is right, and I am free to tell you that my experience disagrees with the advice being given. Happy parenting!

(This page has been left blank for your planning or notes)

CHAPTER 3: TERRIFIC THREES AND THE LITTLE FU**ER FOURS

"Monopolooze. To strategically lose a board game against an un-sportsman-like child." - Dadonymous

In this chapter, we are going to cover the four gruesome things you will encounter in childhood:

- Lying
- Picky eating
- Potty training
- The merits of sleeping habits.

To help you through this stage, I offer you a Mint Coffee (+ bonus coffee carrytail), the House-made Clover Club (& a plethora of variations), plus my favorite the La Fleur (with a variation that has a variation)!

If you are holding your precious child who looks so angelic sleeping only minutes after their overtired tantrum, if you're feeling exhausted, with your last nerve frazzled, at this moment you hate everyone around you for not "getting it", and you are currently desperately seeking some uplifting opening to this chapter from someone who has been there and should "totally get it!"; let me apologize now. That is not what is going to happen here.

Welcome to the age where you still feel like you are literally doing everything twice-over for your littles.

They have grown more independent and are always trying to help. They're not really helping. It is just doubling your workload. Cute as they may be, you long for it to be easy and it is not.

You may want to skip ahead to the recipe section of this chapter, make yourself one, and then you can pick back up here where I will get into the four gruesomely difficult what & why of this age-stage.

GRUESOME THING ONE: LYING

I was unaware of how brazen lying is in kids. I think if you were to ask, maybe someone without children, what kids are well known for, brutal honesty would rank somewhere in the top three.

They'd be wrong.

The more expert research I read from the Canadian Professor of Education and Counselling Psychology, Dr. Talwar, on the deception that small precious children are capable of, the more shockingly relieved I become. Shocked, because they are waaay better at lying than we adults realize. They are so good that hundreds of tests show we can't really tell if in-fact, they are lying. The kicker is - they do it a lot.

WHY RELIEVED?

When your first child blatantly lies to you, and you know you are being lied to, it is a personal affront to your parentage. Talwar has decoded lying as a common milestone in development. In order to lie, they have to be advanced in cognitive and social skill development. Ergo, lying actually equals a sign of intelligence.

Whew. OK, so my lying little angel is just smart, right?

A lot of us would like to believe that our precious babies don't lie. But they do. There is a study commonly called the "peeking game". This is where kids have to guess what toy someone is holding behind the proctors back by sound alone. Conveniently, on the hardest toy to identify by sound, the proctor will leave the room, laying the toy on a table behind the child, and tell the kid not to peek. It is incredibly difficult to not peek because up until this point they have been told how smart they are at this guessing game. It is obvious how pleased the adult is with their stupendous capabilities and the pi'ece de r'esistance is that if they get this one right then they get a prize, and who doesn't want a prize?

33.33% of three-year-old's will peek and subsequently, when confronted about their possible deception, own up to it, but 80% of four-year-old's will peek and then LIE about it afterward.

LIE. Outright LIE!

Most adults chalk this down to innocence, feeling like it is something that will be outgrown and therefore they will choose to ignore the lie because it somewhat feels like a minor infraction.

NOPE. IT AIN'T SO.

Children will become more adept at lying if their lie is ignored and left to fester.

I did not know any of this when my littles were young. In our house, lying was a moral sin that could only be prevented by good adulting. I equated their need to lie to failures as a mother. *Am I alone in this?* I somehow knew internally that heavy punishments breed craftier kids, so I addressed this by saying, "If you tell me the truth, you won't be in trouble and you will feel much better by being honest."

TURNS OUT THAT WAS A MISTAKE.

To be clear, my statement of "if you tell me the truth, you won't be in trouble and you will feel much better by being honest" definitely decreased lying. This is because kids realize that they are free from a punitive measure. However, this only addresses one hard issue of why kids lie, to avoid punishment. There is a secondary reason why that is important in the understanding of why they lie, that is to please their parents.

What I should have said, "If you tell me the truth, you won't be in trouble AND I will be so happy you told me the truth."

WHY THIS WORKS

Parables commonly are a favorite way of teaching the young and old. There are two parables for teaching about lying in a parents' arsenal. The Little Boy Who Cried Wolf and George Washington and the Cherry Tree.

I was shocked to learn, ironically when I read NutureShock by Bronson and Merryman, that only one of these parables is truly effective in reducing lies and one INCREASES IT.

In The Little Boy Who Cried Wolf, the boy receives the ultimate punishment for lying. He gets eaten. Seems like the threat of death would stop anyone, especially kids, from lying.

On the contrary, kids interpret the boy as being inept with his deception and he should have been more covert to avoid such a drastic ending. The morality and negative consequences of lying does not even enter their reasoning. Case studies even cite that when kids are given this parable of the little boy, their frequency of lying goes up substantially.

On the other hand, in Georgie's story, after he confesses, he is rewarded by his dad for telling the truth. The kids in Bronson and Meryman's study, after hearing this story, show that 75% of boys and 50% of girls become honest after their initial deception. Ironically, this whole story of George Washington is a lie. It never even happened. What the implications are for teaching our kids not to lie from a lie afterward has yet to be studied. But, don't let that dissuade you from using the parable, our neighbors to the north in Canada removed the name George Washington altogether, to test for a patriotic effect, and found the story is just as effective with any Tom, Dick or Harry name.

When kids are faced with coming clean without punishment and from this, they know they are making their parents happy, they will tell the truth more often. I know it seems confusing because if they have done something wrong, they should face consequences, right?

Yes, they should face the natural consequences of their actions. However, that is completely different to more punishment piled on top of that. What a parent must choose in these instances is the long game. What are you more concerned with? Most of us would probably answer ensuring our kids don't lie to us.

If this is your answer, then you should look at these moments as an opportunity to build trust in your relationship. This thought change will help your kids know you mean what you say, they can trust that when they screw up, they can come to you, and when they own up to their mistakes it will bring you closer, not further apart.

WHAT ABOUT WHEN THEY ARE OLDER?

Lying becomes a growing symptom from a desire to manipulate and control situations. When kids are rewarded for not being caught in lies, they inevitably also learn that they can cope with the rigors of school and peer pressure by lying. This becomes an easy way to garner attention.

WHAT TO DO ABOUT IT?

Before they reach school-age, all the current research suggests not letting it be an "elephant in the room" problem that is not discussed. Address it as plain as the nose on your face but without anger.

I never said it was an easy fix. I fully respect that this is difficult and often tedious when you have a child in the throngs of a "lying stage". If they have reached school-age and are well into the older child arena, I humbly extend my condolences. You have a long road ahead of you to undo this learned behavior.

It is vital to state that their learned behavior is not always entirely your burden to bear. There are other people in your child's life who teach them how to behave, even if you are weird and unsocialized homeschoolers like my family. Kids learn what they learn from everywhere. It is improbable that one could filter out all bad influences. Our task as parents is to be the constant "guide-on-the-side" pointing to the best way to adult. When you see that they have veered off course, the only way back is to lovingly provide a lit path for them to the right track. This may not happen in your lifetime but keep at it nonetheless, the work is providential.

GRUESOME THING TWO: PICKY EATING, THE RITE OF PASSAGE

It can be one of the most frustrating issues a parent can go through at any age during your child's growth. We are talking about it in this chapter because this is where we usually encounter it first. You know, right when you are encountering everything for the first time, it happens just for kicks when you are the most tired as a parent.

As part of our evolutionary survival growth, we as tiny humans, are designed to crave sweet things because bitter items could be toxic. As such, our taste buds at this age far outnumber what you have after the age of 20. That means that that piece of broccoli really does taste "yucky"!

STACKING THE ODDS

Parenting, like chess, is about knowing your opponent's next possible move. In this case, the most likely move is going to be all the whiney refusals you are going to get.

Some of the best advice I read was from Laura Jana MD in Food Fights. She wrote about stacking the odds in your favor by roasting veggies in an oven, which brings out a vegetable's natural sweetness. Sour will counteract bitter. With brussels sprouts, green beans, zucchini, and broccoli it is massively helpful to squeeze a little lemon juice on them before roasting. Play around with texture, temperature, seasoning, and shapes.

Dietitian Melissa Halas Liang RD wrote about how a lot of kids will refuse to eat cooked peas; however, they will eat them frozen out of a bag. Which is gross to me but hey, they are getting their protein! Imagine what happens when you mash and bake them in a star shape with butter and salt?

Besides cooking or not cooking, to stack the odds you can also play into their egos.

Have your kids help in all areas of family meal prep. Offering them some self-choice in choosing what recipes to break out for the week ahead, choosing what goes on the shopping list and in the cart, and finally cooking for the family. It becomes increasingly more difficult for your child to breakdown into a tantrum about the choices that they personally made.

If, by chance, you're getting tantrums during the choosing, maybe take a break with a cocktail or a carrytail and go for something simpler. Cuddling up with your child in a non-tantrum state to find the recipes (you may need to make one up about cubed cheese, if that is all they like) they love and write down in the margin of the page their opinion with a date attached to it.

What writing this down does is a start to show them that you validate their feelings and thoughts. This tiny gesture will go a long way to knocking down that wall of pickiness they have built.

WHEN IS IT ENOUGH?

The biggest concern for myself was, were they getting enough nutrition? The fact is - eating habits change drastically and quickly. The most important thing to remember is that for each year of age they only need 1 tablespoon of food per meal. So, the one-big-bite rule is sufficient when they are eating five plus times per day.

I wish I knew when I was going through this was the idea to present it, not push it.

It takes roughly fourteen times for a food to be introduced to a kid before they integrate it into their diet. I know that this knowledge at the time would have helped me feel much saner because 14 times is a crazy long time to be patient.

Something else I have since learned is that it is unrealistic to have a toddler sit down for more than 15 minutes for dinner.

Ironically, this is the thing that I teach in all my teaching books; movement is formula for learning. But somehow it got lost in translation for me to apply it to eating times with my own circus. Go figure. So, try shortening dinner times for the kids. Also, try ordering the meal, the first course can be the "try it" round and the second course being the "favorites".

Cornell University has also found research to backup rebranding of 'sucky foods' that preschoolers won't eat with cooler names. Shocker, I know, but perhaps now you will feel validated for calling plain ole carrots, "Night Vision Sticks" *said with a dramatic movie guy's voice.*

ABSOLUTELY AVOID THESE FOUR THINGS

There are four things that I have found in my own experience as a parent and aunt that are detrimental to the development of a child's eating habits.

First, you can't be picky yourself. You need to be open to trying new things too, even if it's just one bite to be polite. They are watching your every move. Show them that it is okay to try new things.

Second, time your dinners away from obvious cranky times. If reading The Art of War has taught me anything it is to pick our battleground terrain. I have no idea if Sun Tzu thought of the parenting applications, but this truly is your greatest advantage in parenting.

Figuring out your family's daunting schedule will be a feat, maybe you sit down earlier or later than you want but trust me when I tell you to start with the advantages in your favor before taking on a toddler.

Third, don't be a short order cook.

If you are always giving in and fixing something separate from the family meal to appease the monster, the monster only grows. Brace yourself with the facts, that they need to have multiple interactions with the food prepared in a variety of ways each time and that just one big bite is enough.

Fourth, don't be militant or over-coddling.

We all know that extremes are limiting and the same applies here. We want to present options without too much attention or demand. If they consistently sit down to a table with a belly ache before even starting to eat, try not to give it too much attention. Nine times out of ten, they are just doing their job and pushing boundaries. If it really is concerning you, then make an appointment with a nutritionist and allergist to rule out the unknown. It is always better to approach a situation with more data.

Food reactions are a real concern.

I have a niece-in-law who is allergic to almost all fruits and vegetables. According to her this has been tested and proven.

I also have an old neighbor whose child eats nothing besides uncooked ramen noodles and a millimeter of egg and toast …how I wish I were joking. Tested and found nothing wrong, not one allergy to medically or logically explain the "severe reactions" to foods.

I ate spinach my whole life until my favorite vegetable turned on me. I was going through a juicing phase and had juiced two pounds of spinach a day for several months until my body shut down and said, "No more!" I thought it was the weirdest thing and kept trying to eat spinach in a variety of ways, but it would not stay put. I finally talked to a nutritionist one year later, *I am a procrastinator I guess*, but I mean who ever heard of a spinach allergy? Well, it exists. And apparently is more common than we know. The reason why I suddenly was having adverse reactions was because I had overtaxed my system. Lesson learned, find out the data before deciding the facts.

CHANGE YOUR ARGUMENT LOCATIONS

A lot of times the only control we have is environmental. Since we humans are creatures of habit, it stands to reason that we might have habitual arguments. It also helps to not always have these arguments in the same setting. If it is always happening at mealtimes, invite the picky kiddo in the kitchen to make dinner with you and have them try it while prepping the family meal.

Sometimes it is okay to relax and give in a little. Instead of responding in a militant fashion, "you are going to eat what the family is eating!", maybe try instead, "you are going to try what the family is having, then you can have something else".

What I have learned from my kids is that over militancy can cultivate an environment for deception. I would always refuse to cook anything in addition to what I had made for the family meal. My practice was "if you don't eat this, you don't eat." My thought process was that they will break down when they get hungry and eat what I had served.

Boy, was I ever mistaken.

Years later, when one is grown and the other is a teen, I find out that they used to sneak down into the kitchen together to get midnight snacks. They were so devious that they rotated and shared a snack so that it was never obvious that anything was ever missing. And though they were terrible at cleaning their rooms, they would clean up spotlessly after themselves so that I never really knew for sure that thievery was going on. Most of the time I thought I was just becoming more forgetful.

I mean, how bad is that? They snuck food at midnight. Yeah, running your house like the military, you just might make future jailbirds.

GRUESOME THING THREE: POTTY-TRAINING

Everyone stops pooping their pants at some point. Some do it at one-years-old while others like to push the boundaries of their parents' sanity and wait until they are five-years-old. What is going to work will be different for every kid. One of mine was easy and the other …

After crying my eyes out over the millionth day of washing sheets in a row, I resolved to resort to magic and consult the farmers' almanac and see what the best days were to train.

I was desperate folks.

When your first child basically trains herself at age one, and the second is already on year two, you begin to question if you really do know what you are doing. As strange as it may seem, the advice I found in reading the Farmer's Almanac for potty-training worked. I guess the moon has some kind of force on the brain-bowel-toilet connection. We immediately called the grandparents and threw an impromptu "pooped in the potty" – party, replete with toys and cake.

Yeah, I used to be cool, but now I get to be excited about poop that I don't have to clean up.

I know if you are sitting there wondering about what to do, there is no magic to potty-training. The most important thing to remember is to breathe, be patient, consistent and model. The one thing you must avoid (as best as you can) is getting angry and being punitive. It will have the opposite effect you desire and there will be consequences for YEARS to come.

If you are getting flack and repeated advice from family, well-meaning friends and random strangers - f**k 'em. They are not the parent, you are. They are not there at three in the morning throwing the last two questionably clean towels over the pee spot, just so you can get another hour of sleep. Breathe and repeat after me, "everyone stops sh*tting their pants at some point." If you feel yourself unable to be patient, close your eyes take a breath deep. Then call your partner or a friend.

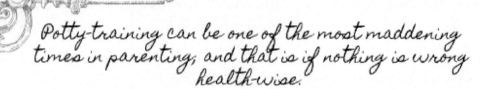

Potty-training can be one of the most maddening times in parenting, and that is if nothing is wrong health-wise.

I can't stress enough about seeking professional help if you seem to have a persistent problem.

There are very real medical problems that your child could be experiencing - to start, look up encopresis and enuresis.

All my thoughts & love are with you - it ain't easy!

GRUESOME THING FOUR: NO SLEEP

When you are a parent, adulting is what happens during the two to three hours after they go to bed. You will be amazed at what you can get done in that short amount of time. But getting your precious little progeny to sleep can be evasive.

Personally, we have had to do everything our imaginations could conjure. The first thing we went with was, in hindsight, probably a mean trick. We would "measure" our children's height short the night before during our bedtime routine and then "surprise! With a little sleep, you are taller!" would await us the next day.

The second thing we tried during this age was more beneficial to all parties involved and it gave them that magical autonomy to learn to control their choices; much better for long-term parenting. We used a technique called "Room Time". This is where we tell them, "you don't have to go to bed, but you do have to go to your room and be quiet." The carrot for them was that they got to choose when sleep worked for them. There were two sticks in this technique. One was us removing their choice if they made noise, they would have to do an unpleasant chore, like sweeping the garage at midnight. The second stick was self-imposing in that, if they chose to stay up late, they would be stealing from their own energy reserves the next day. After a week on their own they inevitably chose to go to bed at a more reasonable hour, but for that week, my garage was spotless! Win – win!

Once your kids find sleep, the peacefulness of the night might be something you easily succumb to and fall asleep yourself; who wouldn't? But what if you can't? What if you need to do some awake-sleep-adulting? This is when it's nice to have yourself a coffee drink… I know that it gives me another two hours to work like Armageddon is coming in the morning.

Easily, the trickiest thing about a child's sleeping habits is how often they change at each stage of development. However, in this chapter-age of toddlers is where the crux of sleep habits develops. We truly had a hard go of it with ours. We never really did everything right, so you know I have some good tidbits on how to build better habits for you from the hindsight of our failures.

WHAT WORKED

It all starts during the day. Throughout the day make sure that your little is getting a lot of fresh air and exercise. Everyday. I know it can be tough with working schedules and often we think that the 20-minute recess should count. Unfortunately, it does not. You need at least a couple of hours outside of unhindered romping.

The architect, Takaharu Tezuka, helped design a kindergarten building in Tokyo, Japan that did not have any boundaries between the inside and the outside world. Some of the amazing data that has come out of observing children interacting there is that they run an average of 4000 meters (2.48 miles), self-imposed every day. What that tells me is that most of our children are not getting enough outside time.

I found that a lot of days I would need to batch outside playtime. Yes, I am that mother that had to schedule playtime. To my chagrin, I would not make it a priority, despite my best intentions unless I had it on a calendar.

Running around outside helps to rebalance the body and reduce stress chemicals (for both of you). Stress chemicals are not the first thing I think of when I think about childhood, much of that is because I am looking back through my adult glasses with an internal comparison of my adult stress to their childhood freedom. However, childhood is stressful in its own way. There are just as many negotiations and relationship steppingstones that they must learn as we have in our adult lives. For them, it might even be more stressful because it is an entirely new schema being developed.

Going outside to play in fresh air helps reduce stress hormones that are running around in a body. This will make it much easier and faster to get them into sleep mode.

I have a lot of friends who rely on a routine to set up bedtime. My question has always been, what happens when that routine is interrupted? Staying at home with one child makes it a little easier to maintain, but if you are traveling, have an event, another kid, family visiting… a lot can happen to mess with your routine.

I want to make it clear that if you have found something that works great for you and you don't want to mess with it, keep at it. I am not the one that is there in the midst of your evening struggles.

There is validity in using a routine as a tool to apply for a season; however long that may last for your family. Perhaps you need to have a routine for a month to ensure you establish sleep patterns, so be it.

When you are establishing sleep, learn the patterns that work with your child's natural cycadean rhythms. Most humans if they experience darkness at 6 pm will naturally get tired. Think about when you are camping away from city lights, the natural darkness causes you to go to sleep earlier.

There is a large portion of the population who think that if they let their kids stay up late, this will cause them to sleep through the night, but surprise… this is not true for many people. That sleep will be hard earned. It will be saturated with cortisol; those are the stress hormones that we just tried to get rid of during our outside time.

If you are shooting for a 7:30 bedtime, start with scheduling their nap time. Make sure that the nap is much earlier in the day. It is completely possible to reset the body's circadian rhythm by dimming the lights and cooling the temperatures in a room by 6 pm. Have a small sugar-free snack in that room while you're reading calming stories. Then a warm bath, and bundled cuddles in bed by 7 pm. 7:30 pm is when you can start to egress the space quietly. Don't be alarmed if there are tears, that is just their way of sharing their fear with you. It is natural and perfectly okay to be afraid. Your parent-job at that moment is to listen and acknowledge their fears.

Sometimes, there are kiddos who just don't do well with you leaving. If that is your case, try being in the room doing quiet things, like folding laundry, reading, or meditation (if you need to have your eyes closed so as not to arouse curiosity). When they are in that ½ sleep they may stir and wake up, but they will be reassured by your presence. Offer a reminder in a soothing voice that it is sleep time. When deep sleep happens, you can leave. This will help them start to associate other things besides touch with security.

One integral thing to keep in mind are the consequences of relying on routines for too long - inflexibility. When we inadvertently nourish inflexibility, we fail to teach the beginning preparations for adulting. The life mantra my dad continually reinforced to my anxiety-ridden self was to remember, "in life we must be so organized we can be flexible".

Enter structure. I know this seems like I am playing a semantics game with you. Structure differs from routine in its strictness. Routine does not abide by any variations on order and time, whereas structure provides a construct with the freedom to move in any direction.

SHARED BED

We haven't even covered the shared bed experience, yet. We had a family bed for six years before my husband called it quits and we started working with the kids to sleep through the night in their own room. I've never regretted having that close bond with our littles, feet in face and all the joys of it.

My advice, do it if you want to, don't if you don't. The essential thing is to know your own limitations as a parent, if you can't function, then don't. If you love it, keep doing it. Or find some A la carte version that fits your family's needs best.

This page has been left blank for your planning or notes

MINT COFFEE
Carrytail | Build | Jam Jar | 1 serving
Wait until bedtime to ask your child to get those undone chores done. Watch how fast they are suddenly ready for bed.

INGREDIENTS
4 oz. strongly brewed coffee or espresso (cooled)
5 – 8 sprigs of fresh mint leaves plus 2 more for garnish
Sweetener (amount of your choice)
1 cup ice
2 tbsp. half and half

STEP 1
In a glass jar, use the bottom of a wooden spoon to muddle *(see pg. 30 for directions)* fresh mint leaves and sugar until the mint is thoroughly bruised and fragrant.

STEP 2
Pour cold espresso (or decaf) over mint mixture and top off with ice, half and half, and your garnish mint leaves. Enjoy!

BONUS RECIPE:
CREOLE LICORICE – Carrytail | Blend | Coffee Mug | 2 cups brewed
I never knew how sassy I was until I started raising miniature humans.

INGREDIENTS
Chicory blend coffee
1.5 tsp. Anise seed
Sweetener (amount of your choice)
0.5 Cup Milk

STEP 1
Brew coffee and anise in basket. While brewing, heat milk up over the stove to just before boiling.

STEP 2
Pour milk into a jar with a lid and shake vigorously until foamy.

STEP 3
Pour coffee into your flashed mug with sweetener, pour frothed milk on top of your coffee and enjoy.

This page has been left blank for your planning or notes)

HOUSE-MADE CLOVER CLUB
Cocktail | Shake | Martini Glass | 1 serving
What I say: "Be ready in five minutes." What my child hears: "Get undressed use your finger paints and lose one shoe."

INGREDIENTS
1.5 oz. Gin
0.5 oz. Dry white vermouth
0.75 oz. Lemon juice
1 tsp. Raspberry preserves
0.25 oz. Egg white
Ice

STEP 1
Place ingredients into your shaker and dry shake (without ice) together vigorously.

STEP 2
Add ice and shake again for a count of 10.

STEP 3
Fine strain into a frosted glass and enjoy!

VARIATIONS:
Try any of your favorite preserves. I say preserves because it's fancier and better than saying simply jelly. Also, try vodka or tequila in place of the gin for a new and inviting kick.

This page has been left blank for your planning or notes

LA FLEUR

Cocktail | Shake | Coupe Glass | 1 serving

Stop drop and ninja yourself — this is how you move with stealth like abilities when checking on your sleeping baby and their stupid-cute eyes pop open.

INGREDIENTS
1 oz. Hendriks gin
1 oz. Elderflower liqueur
2 oz. Fresh grapefruit juice + thinly peeled rind
Ice

STEP 1
Pour in your liquid ingredients into the shaker with two handfuls of ice.

STEP 2
Cover and shake vigorously for 10 shakes

STEP 3
Fine strain from shaker into your frosted glass.

STEP 4
Take your thinly peeled grapefruit rind, squeeze it and with a sweeping motion go back and forth over your glass.

The grapefruit needs to be thinly sliced because the white pith will turn your drink bitter. I like to use a vegetable peeler, then clean up the edges of the peal with a paring knife.

When I was first taught to do this, I thought it was bogus! But I have had the drink without doing that last flourish and the entire olfactory experience was missing. A good cocktail can be made to taste good to your taste buds. However, a great cocktail will entertain your sniffer first before it hits your palette. This sweeping motion of the peel distributes the oils, giving your drink a faint flowery hint of grapefruit when finished place peel inside your decadent libation.

COCKTAIL VARIATIONS:
EAST SIDE ELDER

INGREDIENTS
2 oz. Austin Reserve gin
1 oz. St. Germain
0.75 oz. Lime juice
5 Mint leaves
3 Slices cucumber
Ice

STEP 1
Muddle *(see pg. 30 for directions)* mint and cucumber in shaker with a wooden spoon handle.

STEP 2
Add other ingredients and fill shaker with ice.

STEP 3

Shake for a count of ten and strain into a frosted glass. Garnish with the top of a mint sprig and a long cucumber slice to enjoy.

Why do I choose brand specific gins? Hendricks is important to use with the grapefruit version of the la fleur because of the flowery profile, however, in this second variation, I'd switch to Austin reserve. This is the gin infused with grapefruit, peppercorns, and lemongrass changing the floweriness to an earthier version.

VARIATION of the VARIATION:

Replace the lime juice with 0.5 oz lemon juice and 1.5 oz fresh squeezed orange juice. Use a thin orange peel to sweep essential oils like you did with the grapefruit in the La Fleur and then toss in for garnish.

HOW OTHER PARENTS DO IT:

Separate But Equal Nightmares

"Put a leash on that kid. Either my kids love to wait until I am distracted with shopping or they themselves get distracted and wander off. I have tried everything, having a plan for when we are separated, lectures, consequences, hold my hand, hold my belt loop, but to no freaking avail. Whatever the reason I am living this personal hell, I've resolved myself to leashing them. I'd rather face any nay-saying-super-parent (& drink a cocktail after that judgment) than lose my kids."
-Safa Houston, TX mom of two - one 6-year-old girl (on the spectrum) and one 2-year-old boy.

"We are a world-schooling family and therefore travel extensively and exhaustively. My weirdo four-year-old loves to hide on the metro. The last time he hid we were in China, and it was sardinely-packed the way only Asian transportation can be. He called out 'Next stop is ours!' my older ones BLINDLY get off! They are out the door when I am frantically calling for them to get back on furiously searching for my hiding little ~~shit~~ brat. When I find him, the doors are, of course, closing and my older ones are NOT back on. So, I mommy-slam the doors and screech out for help. Thankfully, an older gentleman, who obviously has finished raising his kids, had the clear headedness to push the emergency button sans judgment in my direction. The crowd shamed my little one forward to where I was exasperatedly standing.

Now we have a 2-part separation rule. Stay where you are, I will come find you. If you are on the car alone get off at the next stop and stay put. So far it is working.

Whatever rules you decide on as a parent. I urge you to have it in place and rehearse it many, many, many times, before EVERY outing."
- Nalina currently in Singapore - single mom of three mostly good kids.

(This page has been left blank for your planning or notes)

CHAPTER 4: FRIENDLY FIVES AND SECRETIVE SIXES

"You have mistaken their cuteness for weakness. They will terrorize you and tear your house upside down like the tiny tornadoes they really are." -Dadonymous

In this stage of your parenting, you have a sweet, cute as a button five-year-old who might suddenly turn into a secretive six-year-old. What happened? We are going to get into that in this chapter as well as the following:

- Walking the fine line between giving away your authority and breaking their spirit
- How to authentically listen (& what the heck is it!)
- Good questions the what, why and how

After we cover all those tough parenting jobs, we will raise our glasses to the Constantinople Coffee (+bonus!), the famous Moscow Mule and her lesser known but equally delicious nine variations.

I remember sitting in my friend's office who, thankfully, also happened to be a therapist, stressing over thinking that I might be breaking my child's spirit by asking her to put on her cardigan before going out into the cold. I equally stressed about my youngest one's intelligence because he constantly asked the same questions over and over.

It felt like I was living in a chaotic circus of my own making. I didn't know which end was up or how to get out of it. Every parenting choice felt vital. This is the age of memory, you know, most humans can remember when they were five and six. Do you know how much that freaked me out?

Essentially the pressure I put on myself was that whatever parenting trap I decided to roll with was going to be the tone for the rest of their life. It would inevitably be how my children started every story about me in the future, "my mom used to…". I became this ridiculous version of myself frozen like a deer-in-the-headlights with simple choices.

He told me to chill.

"Seriously, Nicole. You are making mountains out of molehills. Look, just decide which arguments are worth having. If you still find yourself frozen with indecision, then look at what is really a life or death choice for you. The cardigan… she will get cold and probably argue less about using it in cold weather next time. Make her hold your hand when crossing the road because that truly is life or death choice. And as far as your younger one goes, that is his way of keeping the conversation going. He wants to talk with you, he wants to know you are listening and there for him. So, keep answering."

Right now, at the tender age of five and six, it is true, the way you engage your child will set the stage for how honest of a relationship you will have with them when they are in their (dreaded) teens.

My struggle was figuring out how to do these things without giving away my authority or breaking their spirit? The two material questions I began asking myself were (1) How do you listen? and (2) How do you control them?

The challenge I needed to embrace with my first child was not being afraid of the chaos that surrounded us. Every rebellious act she committed - not cleaning her room, not putting on warmer clothes, not crossing the road safely, created chaos in our family. These choices, which spun our lives out of control, I learned to realize that they were learning opportunities disguised. This was where she was learning full autonomy of her world. My job was to make sure she was safe. And beyond that, let her fail so that she could learn.

FYI, this has never ended, she is still pushing my comfort zone as a baby-adult in all things and I still must watch her fail and then get up to try something new.

If she knows she is safe to try, she will. The trying will teach her real authentic life lessons that will stick with her forever. Knowing she is safe to do so with me, will also teach her that I will be the guide-on-the-side to help when and if she needs it.

My youngest has taught me how vital authentic listening is in any relationship.

WHAT IS AUTHENTIC LISTENING

Authentic Listening is where you are not waiting for your turn to talk. You are diving deep into their world of story, listening to their thoughts without judgment, and without checking out. Then, perhaps most importantly, repeating what you hear before responding.

Surprisingly, conversation is one of the hardest things for our brains to do. It requires our frontal lobe, the front part of our brain that is supposed to be responsible for: reasoning, judgment ...*this is probably broken for me!...*, and social interaction, to be continuously engaged. This is not a simple task, it requires the brain to be focused for a sustained period, ensuring that it does not go into autopilot; which is where I tend to go if I hear anything about any video game ever.

HOW TO AUTHENTICALLY LISTEN

Yes, it is labor intensive but well worth the effort. I started practicing this with my youngest in his diatribes of these pretend worlds he would want to include me in. Then, I learned that it could also be used as an effective diffusion tool for arguments between my kids or with their friends.

Recently, I saw a girlfriend of mine that I have known since fifth grade, she did a version of authentic listening in her day-to-day conversations with her three-year-old child. I was elated that she had discovered this tool early on in her parenting; one that had taken me nearly a decade to really figure out. When I shared my excitement with her, she confessed she had recently been chastised by another fellow mom-friend saying the "repeating of words" was putting words into her child's mouth and not helping him grow his language skills.

F**k, if we aren't judged by everyone.

I obviously disagree. I, along with research, have found it is helping him put his thoughts to words and connect to his feelings. She is not telling him how to feel, she is letting him know he is heard and understood. This is one of the top seven desires of our hearts, to be heard and understood. Mark and Debra Laaser are counselors and authors of the incredible book, <u>The Seven Desires of the Heart</u>. In their book, they draw lessons from all their years of counseling couples and individuals. They crafted a list of the seven common hurts that they noticed reoccurring in their sessions, from patients who would mention that they struggled with never having them in their current relationships or didn't have them growing up.

Throughout this book, in each chapter, I cover how we as parents can be providing these inherent desires so that our children are not seeking them from other avenues. But because I know you are dying for an exact list ...*at least I know I would be!..* here they are: (1) To be heard and understood, (2) To be affirmed – this is praise for what you do, (3) To be blessed – this is loved for what you already are, (4) To be safe – emotionally secured, (5) To be touched – all of the hugs and cuddles, (6) To be chosen – being accepted, (7) To be included – a part of something bigger, a community.

Earlier in the week of writing this chapter, my baby-adult daughter came to me frustrated that her friends didn't know or care how to take the time to really listen to each other and what was being said. She said, "Why did you raise me this way, no one else knows how to talk this way. I know how good it feels to really be heard, but all these people don't. I feel like I have a full-time job mediating between my girlfriends."

Me too kid.

Not to get all Gandhi on you guys but, the change must come from within first. If you want to teach good listening, be a good listener. To help your child prioritize their feelings and self-soothe, you need to use this process in your daily life. Throughout their childhood, they will come to realize that there is at least one person in this world who understands. This will be the framework you need when they are teens who would rather not tell you anything. Eventually, they will remember that you are the safe harbor by which to discuss their inner hearts.

Below I am listing the steps for authentic listening in case you want to write them down on a notecard and break it back out when you need them most.

What? …Am I the only one that needs memory aids?

In the heat of the moment, it is often difficult to suss out what is really bothering your child and communicate on their level without triggered emotion. Let's face it, heated moments are full of racing emotion from all parties involved. Even if your role is playing mediator your children can rile up your emotions like a roller coaster. They know your buttons better than you do. I guess my buttons get pushed easily, I will often whip out a note card to ensure I follow my steps. Ridiculous, yes… but so what, parenting is hard and so is memory.

6 Authentic Listening Steps for Conversation Tactics:

    1. Listen to what they are telling you
    2. Repeat back what you hear.
    3. Let them correct if needed.
    4. Repeat back correction.
    5. Speak to the thought.
    6. Ask a question that pertains to the thought. (Not a leading question)

What is a leading question? This is a question that either requires a "yes" or "no" answer or one that contains information that the asker is looking to have confirmed. A solid way to identify a leading question is if it has too many variables that probably need to be individually addressed.

Let's say you have two children fighting, both come in crying-yelling-upset-blaming each other. One has a red face and says, "they hit me", then you ask, "did you hit XXXX in the face with your fist?" The problem with any answer to this question is two-fold. One, it won't give you enough background information to go on because it will either be a "yes" or "no". Secondly, the question assumes what you have previously concluded the answer before knowing all the facts.

How to ask this differently: Try an open-ended question, "XXXX, can you tell me what you think happened?" An open-ended question gives space for them to give the answerer to their side of a situation. This helps them feel heard. In all conflict, regardless of fault, everyone wants to, at least, feel heard. This helps the child to verbally process their thinking, which if they are at fault, often after saying it aloud they are able to see it from another person's perspective, gain sympathy and accept responsibility for their part. If that doesn't happen, you as the listener will be able to better understand how they process choices in the heat of their emotions and learn which life-skills they need help working on.

Just as important as knowing what steps to do, is to always include the three things that you should avoid doing while practicing conversation. This is fundamentally a new way to have a discussion and it may require breaking old habits. These three "don'ts" are what will keep you from being present and listening (and are commonly done by almost everyone!):

1. Don't plan your argument while listening
2. Don't hang on to what you want to say
3. Don't simply wait for your turn to talk

WHAT CAN A GOOD QUESTION DO?

Turns out that the most important thing to do as a parent is to make sure your kid knows they are safe with you. When we ask questions that show interest, we are demonstrating that we care and are truly listening to our little persons. This cultivates an understanding of "I am safe" to your child.

You want that.

During life's chaos, you want them to know that you are genuinely interested in what they are thinking. Paving the way for them to know that you are the one to go to, you are the one making an effort for their attention, and asking good questions is your starting ground.

(This page has been left blank for your planning or notes)

CONSTANTINOPLE COFFEE
Carrytail | Brew | Coffee Mug | 4 cup servings
Parenthood powered by love, fueled by coffee, and sustained by cocktails.

INGREDIENTS
0.25 tsp. Ground cinnamon
0.25 tsp. Freshly ground black peppercorns
0.25 tsp. Ground ginger
0.25 tsp. Ground nutmeg
1/8 tsp. Freshly ground green cardamom seeds
1/8 tsp. Ground cloves

STEP 1
Brew spices and ground coffee in your coffee pot.

STEP 2
Fix your coffee in your mug as usual. Enjoy!

BONUS RECIPE:
CAFÉ PICANTE – Carrytail | Brew | Coffee Mug | 4 cups brewed
What if I told you that your dad (…that you just walked past…) could also make you a sandwich?

INGREDIENTS
1 tsp. Ground cinnamon
0.5 tsp. Chili powder
0.25 tsp. Cayenne pepper
0.25 Cup Heavy cream
1 Tbsp. Unsweetened cocoa powder
1 Tbsp. Confectioners' sugar

STEP 1
Brew coffee, cinnamon, chili and cayenne in a basket together.

STEP 2
While coffee is brewing, whip heavy cream, cocoa, and sugar together until soft peaks form.

STEP 3
After coffee is brewed and poured into flashed mugs, divide the whipped cream into each mug and enjoy.

This page has been left blank for your planning or notes

MOSCOW MULE
Cocktail | Build | Copper Mug | 1 serving
How can I start out the day like Mary friggen Poppins only to end the day like Cruella Deville?

INGREDIENTS
1.5 oz. Vodka
1 Lime juiced + 1 wedge for garnish
Ginger beer
Ice

STEP 1
Juice one lime in your copper mug

STEP 2
Add your measure of vodka

STEP 3
Fill mug with ice to the top

STEP 4
Add ginger beer until full and garnish with a wedge of lime. Enjoy!

Why the copper mug?
When copper encounters a pH acidity less than 6 (lime juice is a pH of 2.0 - 2.4) it releases and gives the Moscow Mule its notorious flavor. However mass consumption of copper (30ml or more) could lead to poisoning. You can use a glass or a lined copper mug if you are concerned about the chemophobic fear-mongering that has been in the news - or if you plan on drinking only Moscow Mules all night after leaving the lime and ginger beer in the copper vessels for HOURS.

COCKTAIL VARIATIONS:

V1: THE KENTUCKY MULE
Using a copper mug, swap out vodka for bourbon, and add a sprig of mint to your lime garnish.

V2: THE DONKEY SHOW …*I know. I know.* If it's too crude for you just call it a Tijuana Mule
This time swap out your copper mug for a good old-fashioned jam jar, and instead of vodka use tequila. Garnish with mint.

V3: SPICY MULE
Using a jam jar or Collins glass, keep the vodka but add an orange liqueur (e.g., Cointreau or Grand Marnier work well). Slice 5 thin pieces of jalapeno. Use three to muddle *(see pg. 30 for directions)* with your measure of lime juice and two slices of jalapenos for garnish.

V4: IRISH MULE
You have probably guessed the variation already, it's Irish whiskey. This offers a sweet undertone similar to the bourbon variation. Carefully choose your ginger beer for this drink, make sure it is dry and spicy. If you're feeling lucky add a dash of green dye. Especially, if its St. Paddy's day - just

kidding… no one who is actually Irish does that. (Use of a copper mug is still suggested)

V5: LONDON MULE
In a Collins glass or jam jar swap your vodka for gin. Traditionalist will insist on a London dry gin and if that is what you have, go for it. I, however, can't stand the taste of dry gin and prefer to use Austin Reserve gin (yes, I'd choose it over Hendricks for this recipe because of the difference in the infusions used for flavorings), it has undertones of grapefruit, lemongrass, and peppercorns… I mean it is heaven in a bottle for mixing with cocktails. Garnish this one with a sprig of mint.

V6: SWEET KREMLIN MULE
This beauty is perfect for summer. Everything stays the same as the original recipe, only add two to three strawberries in to muddle *(see pg. 30 for directions)* with your measure of lime juice and a few extra slices to adorn your jam jar or Collins glass.

The last three recipes get a little more eccentric in their changes but are well worth the effort.

V7: THE LAVENDER MULE [Stir]
2 oz vodka
1 oz St. Germain's
2 oz ginger beer
2 tablespoons of culinary lavender to make a lavender syrup *(see pg. 20 for syrup directions)*
Edible flower (pansy, nasturtiums, lavender, begonias)
Ice cubes

In a mixing glass pour all of your ingredients and stir, then strain over ice into your chilled coupe glass. Garnish with an edible flower.

V8: GLASGOW MULE
1.5 oz. Scotch whisky
0.5 oz. St. Germain's
0.75 oz lemon juice
1 dash Angostura bitters
4oz Ginger beer
Ice
Lemon peel
Candied ginger (this is usually found in your grocer's dried fruit section)

Pour all ingredients, except your ginger beer, into your cold copper mug, then top off with ice. Next, pour in your ginger beer and garnish with a twisted lemon peel and candied gingers that has been skewered on a long enough pick. What is "long enough"? Something that allows the garnish to rest on top of the concoction.

V9: THE GARDEN MULE [Shake]
12 Blueberries
4 ¼ inch thick slices of Cucumber

1oz Lime juice
2oz Vodka
4oz Ginger beer
6 mint leaves and 1 sprig
Candied ginger
Ice

In the bottom of your shaker muddle *(see pg. 30 for directions)* together all cucumber, 8 blueberries, 6 mint leaves. Next, pour in lime juice and vodka and a handful of ice, shake vigorously for a count of 10. Strain into chilled copper mug full of ice and top off with ginger beer. Finally skewer 2 blueberries, candied ginger piece, 2 more blueberries. Garnish alongside a sprig of mint.

HOW OTHER PARENTS DO IT:

Always Check Pockets Before You Launder.

"I have seven children. Six boys and one girl. It took me until child number three to figure this out. Guess I am a slow learner. They have put all kinds of things into their pockets. Crayons, rockets, knives, dirt. The fourth one is a real pocket stuffer. I am certain he is on this earth to make sure I learn to make THEM empty THEIR own pockets before throwing clothes into the laundry basket. I figured this out after I washed two lizards and a frog. Trust me, you don't want to find this either while you are sorting dirty clothes, or afterward IN THE DRYER!!! After this crimson Shakespearean tragedy, I was wishing for the days of "just" melted crayons."

– Cindy, mom of 7 - New Orleans, LA

This page has been left
blank for your planning
or notes)

CHAPTER 5: SOCIABLE SEVENS AND EFFUSIVE EIGHTS

"Please don't compare your dog problems to parenting. Your dog doesn't say your name 3852 times a day." -Momonymous

In this chapter, while we are parenting our party-time seven-year-olds and our expressively grateful eight-year-olds, we are going to dive into:

- A world of make believe
- The ADHD problem that isn't
- Opposing opinions
- When they learn by doing

Of course, after hearing anyone's opinions we are going to need some delicious concoctions; Tajin Lasse (+ variations), a traditional Margarita with variations and 4 surprising twists: the Lagerita, Daisy Verde, Agave 2 Ways, and the Grapefruit Dazy.

I remember at this age my children started to question what reality was and what make-believe was. Before the ages of seven and eight, I lived in this magical world where everything was possible. Trolls, dragons, fairies, Santa, Krampus, unicorns all lived there with us.

I didn't know how much it would hurt to fall out of the clouds until my first-born pushed me there. The day came when she asked me one question was all she asked, "Is the Easter bunny real?", I was overwhelmed with the intensity of this childhood-ending moment. Trying to face the truth in her large watery blue eyes felt invasively vulnerable to me.

My father had always taught me that when kids ask, the best course of action is to go with the plain and simple truth. Regardless of how brutal it feels to cut away the ~~lie~~ fantasy. That is your one and only moment to sew trust with them.

This newly sewn trust is what you will need to reap years later when they are teens and secretly or not so secretly rebelling.

"No, he isn't." I could feel my body begin to vibrate with intensity; like the rug was about to be pulled out from under me.
"Is Santa?"
"No."
"The tooth fairy?"
… Mercy, kid! One thing at a time. Why do we have to do this now? The whole world is falling down. It's over! The curtain of childhood is being pulled back… "No."
"Why'd you tell me it was? Why are you crying, mommy?"

I had not even realized that tears were running down my face. "Because I wanted… I wanted…to help you develop your imagination… Are you angry with me for pretending?"

"No, it was fun. Why are you sad?"
"Because you are growing up so fast, it is hard to catch up to you."

I'm "so extra", or at least that is how my teens like to currently describe me. Her dad and I had played elaborate ruses to keep the magic alive for years. She wanted to know how we had accomplished it all. After telling her everything in grave detail, we asked her, "Do you want to help us with your younger brother?"

"YES! That would be fun."

I had another five-bliss-filled-magical-years and now with a new partner-in-crime. These last five years were beautiful. But much the same way, and at the same tender age of eight, my youngest asked me the unveiling question and my pretend world ended.

IT'S EASY TO JUDGE HISTORY'S PAST THROUGH PRESENT UNDERSTANDING.

Thirteen years is a good run of make-believe. Though, I question the bitter sweetness of having arrived in the future and not being able to go back to tell my past self that it was worth it. Some of my parent-friends totally disagree with me, they feel like the make-believe years set up a manipulative trap of mistrust. Possibly. Still, what's done is done and I cherish those memories.

Whatever you choose, to play pretend, or stay in the absolute truth of it all, remember that you will always need to sew trust with your child. That's the big take away. When they ask, tell.

ADHD - EVOLUTION'S FAULT

This is a common age when parents, teachers, and the world will notice if a child seems to be particularly hyper in their activity.

It happened to me in the 1980s, my parents were called into a meeting where they discussed my poor behavior, my inability to stop fidgeting and my overall lack of focus. There was a new drug at the time that they thought they might like to try on me that had shown to help kids calm down. My parents said, "no, thanks" and filled my life with doing multiple sports every. single. season. began.

I never knew until I was getting ready to go to university that I had this problem. My dad pulled me aside and said, "Look, kid, you have a lot of energy and it really is best for you if you have some sort of physical activity to help you focus." As he went into more detail, my past became crystal clear.

As I type this, my husband is noticing my legs are shaking and is asking me if I want to go on our evening walk. I often drive my friends crazy with my "nervous energy". I love to host gatherings and right before the storm of guests' arrivals usually one or two really good girlfriends will come over to help me sort out the pre-party To-Do's. They invariably mistake my surge of energy for something negative, but it is how I get it all done. I get that during these times I am not pleasant to be around, and most need to make allowances for me. Thankfully, they have found a way to love me in spite of myself.

This by no means is a commentary on not using drugs to better enhance a life-experience. It is merely my history.

I have an old friend who wasn't diagnosed with ADD until adulthood, she was prescribed medication and almost overnight became more successful at her job and marriage. Do what works for you. For me, it is scheduling a lot of breaks and trying to remember to work out; for others, medicine is the answer.

What I do want to call attention to is that this is not necessarily a new problem – and do we even want to consider it a problem at all?

There has been substantial research showing how since the dawn of hunter-gathers there are those who are more hyper than others. Could the problem lie in the way we expect children to behave and learn?

If you recall the architect Tezuka, who designed a kindergarten school in Tokyo from chapter two. His building focused on erasing the boundary between the outside and the inside. The school adapted a mantra of freedom for their students. If a child leaves the classroom to go explore elsewhere, it must be because he has extra energy to expel. They let him do this rather than forcing him to "behave", they trust that he will come back when ready. The ones that wander off do inevitably come back with little disruption to the rest. I told you in chapter two how the average kid runs 2.48 miles a day in that school, however, I didn't tell you one of the most surprising group of kids. There are a few who have been tracked running 6000m (3.72 miles) just in the morning. Imagine trying to contain that little Nicole! The only idea that I am suggesting with here is that all children seem to need a lot more movement than we are currently providing and some even more than others – what would change if we changed our expectation views on what is "good behavior" from a child? How would they internalize that blessing of being accepted for who they are?

If you are going through parenthood with a hyper child, just know that a gazillion others have faced this too, you are not alone and there is nothing wrong with your kid. This will be one more area where you will need to find adjustments to make it all work. Just like the parent next door.

THE COMING AGE OF OPINIONS

Opposing sentiments from children are stressful. It can cause the home to feel out of harmony. Terrible timing on their part as our kids, when a safe place full of peace is the very thing you or they need. Almost half of parent's rate arguments with their kids as feeling destructive to the very relationships they are trying to build.

Most of us are doing everything we can to protect and raise healthy well-adjusted kids, but when your authority is being challenged it is easy to feel like you are also being disrespected.

Set down your heavy burden, more than 82 % of kids just don't see arguments that way, (no, I am not making this statistic up). Astonishingly, kids thought it strengthened their understanding of their parents' points of view.

Of course, not all fighting equals arguments and not all arguments equal understanding.

The kind of disagreements, even if they are heated disagreements, that bring about a strengthening in the relationship and an articulated understanding are the ones that allow for give and take. The ones where both sides have listened to one another. Just as importantly both sides feel that their points of view were heard and considered. Afterward, both parties are able to then reach a compromise. These are the kind of fights that are healthy for growing families to go through.

At this point, you might be feeling as though the research is duplicitous. First, as a parent, you have to set clear expectations and follow through. On the other hand, you are supposed to allow for arguments and concessions?

Welcome to fu**ing parenting.

How are you as a parent supposed to retain any legitimacy and trust in what you say if you allow for the kids to argue their way to what they want? I know. It confused me too and looking back I am not sure that I "get it".

Here is my current takeaway, have very few rules guidelines that you can enforce in two ways. First, you have the reasoning behind why the guidelines exist for your family (e.g., inside versus outside voices). When you establish the value behind the expected behavior you are helping them start to think for themselves by building understanding behind the rule. The opposite end of the parenting spectrum would be expecting blind obedience to "my rules" and the "do it because I said so" kind of parenting.

WHY ISN'T MY COMMAND ENOUGH?

My question right back at'cha would be, "Do you want sheep who blindly follow a leader or children with the ability to process with original self-thinking - especially when they are out with their friends?"

See where I am going with this? When my kids were at this age, we totally bought into the dominance parenting style. Mostly because we were tired, and we just wanted to have "it" done and not "argue" about it. Then the epiphany came that we were modeling their future decisions and inadvertently stifling their creative thinking, brewing our own rebellious little circus. We course corrected; departing from our "Sage on the Stage" nature, to exerting more patience and squeezing ourselves into the mold of "Guide on the Side" parents who took more time to explain our values behind our expectations and guidelines. Slowly helping our offspring to begin to see reason and develop their maturity.

The second part of my takeaway is that you have "go to" consequences for when these guidelines are or are not followed. If you are newly adjusting to this style of parenting, I'd recommend sitting down with a partner and list the good and bad consequences to each expectation. Then laminate it, put it on the fridge (maybe make a note card or two for your wallet, purse, and pocket ...*what? I totally can't rely on my memory! Environmental Engineering, baby!*) to refer to during the doling out of rewards or corrections.

Most importantly, be flexible. When your kids give you strong arguments for special circumstances, truly consider what they are asking. This lets your little ones know, no bullsh*t when you say something you mean it, but also you respect their opinion and if they have thought it out and have sound reasoning, you are gentle enough to listen.

Hopefully, that will translate to your future teen being more honest with you than not.

LEARNING CHANGES

Previously, I mentioned how children zero to four-years-old learn best, through a response social feedback loop (talking to them about what they are pointing, looking, babbling towards). However, when you are parenting a child between the ages of 5 to 12 years of age, you need to add in more and more opportunities to learn by doing it themselves. This transition can also be the moments that require the greatest deal of patience from you. It is incredibly easy for you with your daily time constraints to just go ahead and do the task. However, consider that the only reason it is easier for you is because someone in your past let you "do" it.

Our main goal in parenting is to always find more ways to grow self-reliance in our children. This is the actual tool they will need to be successful adults. Letting your kids "do" rather than "watch or listen" is how to ensure that they build the confidence they need in their own abilities to trust what they can and cannot do.

HOW DOES THIS LOOK IRL (in real life)?

When they want to jump from tree log to another too far away tree log, let them do it. Let them find out that they can or can't by falling. Instead of loudly sucking in all of your breath at the too close to the open oven door while "helping" you prepare family dinners, remind them in a serious lowered tone of voice that it is "hot" and to "think first", with any luck they are like 99.7% (yes, this is a made-up statistic) of humanity and won't allow themselves to get hurt too badly.

These lowered voice reminder moments are when you are helping them to slow down their thought processes and become more self-aware. When you have their attention, try saying, "what do you think I am going to ask/remind/tell you?" instead of the often-exasperated expressions that come tumbling out of the majority of us parents:

- "What are you doing?!"
- "What were you thinking?!"
- "Stop it!"
- "NO! Get Back!"
- "What is the matter with you?!"
- "You know better!"

The difference is that you are asking them to think instead of supplying the answer for them. Let's not be under any false pretenses, learning often happens at slower-than-a-turtle-pace and with a gazillion repeated offenses. One crucial element to incorporate right after you ask, "what do you think I am going to remind you of?" that will ensure lasting results in their learning, to wait. Wait. WAIT. (yep, sometimes it will take an incessantly long time) for them to answer your query without you prodding or supplying hints to them to make the answer come out quicker. Try to take a breath and remember that their answering you is not your goal but helping their brains to reinforce the memory route to the possible consequences is what you are working towards.

Though it is counter-intuitive and dangerous, let them hold a super sharp knife free from your adroit hands and let them chop the nuts for the dinner salad – it really is a good parenting technique and how they will best learn. These teachable moments are where you are garnering confidence in their own abilities by letting them do, which is far more effective than you simply telling them they are capable. Secondly, this doing is going to help them learn quicker what not to do than all of your fretting, lecturing, gasping at the almost worst-case scenario that just flashed before your eyes while they "help".

I promise.

This page has been left blank for your planning or notes

TAJIN LASSE
Carrytail | Blend | Poco Grande Glass | 4 servings
Getting your child's attention is much easier by sitting down and looking comfortable.

INGREDIENTS
0.5 Cup Lemon juice + lemon peel
3 Bananas peeled
0.25 Cup Coconut cream
0.25 Cup Sugar
Ice
Cherry
Sugar & Tajin spice (usually found in the "Mexican" or "international" aisle of your grocery store) for rim garnish

STEP 1
Rim glasses with cut lemon. On a small plate combine sugar and tajin. Dip the rim of your glass in this mixture to coat the exterior. Set in freezer to frost while you blend your carrytail.

STEP 2
Fill blender with ice, juice, bananas, sugar, and cream, blending until smooth. Garnish with lemon peel and cherry on a toothpick and enjoy!

VARIATIONS:
Substitute bananas for mangos, strawberries, or blueberries.

This page has been left
blank for your planning
or notes

MARGARITA
Cocktail | Shake or Blend | Margarita Glass | 1 serving
For that awkward moment when you realize you just punished your kid for acting just like you.

INGREDIENTS
Frozen:
1.5 oz. Tequila blanca
0.5 oz. Orange liqueur
¼ cup frozen limeade (concentrate)
0.5 cup of ice for blending
Chunky salt + small saucer for salt
Blender
Frosted Coupe or jar

On the Rocks:
1.5 oz. Tequila blanca
0.5 oz. Orange liqueur
0.5 oz. Lime juice + thinly sliced lime wheel for garnish
0.5 oz. Agave nectar
Ice for cup and shaking
Chunky salt + small saucer for salt
Shaker
Frosted Coupe or jar

STEP 1
Determine if you want your drinks on the rocks or frozen. Either put your liquids into the shaker (on the rocks) or blender (frozen)

STEP 2
Determine if you like your margarita a little sweeter. I am a sucker for a sweet/tart flavor, so I always use frozen limeade. If you prefer something less sweet, then just use a limeade juice, not from concentrate.

STEP 3
Cut your lime into quarters and run the pulp part around the outside of your frosted glass.

STEP 4
Salting your glass. Place a small amount of salt into a saucer, using just the wetted exterior lip of your glass dip your glass into your salt saucer. Place the glass back into the freezer until you finish crafting your cocktail.

STEP 5
Add your ice and either shake 10 times or blend for 30 seconds on high (until smooth).

STEP 6

If you are having your margarita on the rocks, fill your glass with ice cubes and strain from your shaker. If you are having it frozen, pour immediately into your glass and enjoy.

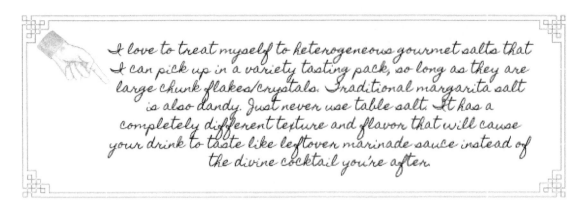

I love to treat myself to heterogeneous gourmet salts that I can pick up in a variety tasting pack, so long as they are large chunk flakes/crystals. Traditional margarita salt is also dandy. Just never use table salt. It has a completely different texture and flavor that will cause your drink to taste like leftover marinade sauce instead of the divine cocktail you're after.

COCKTAIL VARIATIONS:
THE SPICY RITAS

LEVEL ONE SPICE: instead of using a lime wedge to wet the outer rim of your glass use the juice from a jar of Trappey's Hot Peppers. Pour a teaspoon of the brine into your margarita and stir. Garnish with a slice of jalapeno with your lime wedge.

LEVEL TWO SPICE: muddle *(see pg. 30 for directions)* or blend ½ a jalapeno with lime juice before adding your spirits. Salt and garnish the same as level one spice.

LEVEL THREE SPICE: infuse your tequila with several jalapenos for at the very least 3 days, the longer you go the spicier it gets. Follow all the steps of the traditional margarita but garnish the same as level one spice.

THE LAGERITA

2 oz. Tequila blanca
0.75 oz. Orange Liqueur
1 oz. Lime juice
4 oz. light Mexican beer (I am a fan of Modelo Especial or Corona Extra)
Ice

First frost your glass in the freezer, then rim the outside with lime juice and dab the outside rim (only) in the salt and put it back in the freezer.

Second, add all ingredients EXCEPT your beer into your shaker with a handful of ice and shake vigorously for a count of 10.

Third, strain into your frosted and salted margarita glass and top off with 4 ounces of beer. Garnish with a lime wheel and enjoy.

DAISY VERDE
1-inch wedge of poblano pepper (+ 1 thin horizontal slice for garnish)
0.75 oz. Pineapple caramel (recipe follows)
2 oz. Tequila blanca
0.5 oz. Lime juice
Pinch of pink Himalayan salt
Sparkling water
Ice

First, to make your pineapple caramel you are going to follow the same instructions as we did for the simple syrup *(see pg. for 30 directions)*. However instead of water use pineapple juice. Also, you are going to boil this (stirring constantly) for longer, until it starts to turn a beautiful caramel color. Remove from heat and let cool (can be stored for up to three months in the refrigerator).

Second, muddle *(see pg. 30 for directions)* the poblano wedge and pineapple caramel in the bottom of your shaker.

Third, add the rest of the ingredients with ice and shake vigorously for a count of 10 and strain into a frosted glass with ice.

Fourth, top with sparkling water and garnish with poblano slice to enjoy.

AGAVE 2 WAYS

2 oz. Tequila blanca
1 small lime
Blood orange soda
Black lava salt
Agave nectar to rim glass
Ice

First, take your frosted martini glass and rim just the outside top edge with agave nectar, then dip the outside rim into your pile of black lava salt. Take precautions to just have the salt on the outside rim, if it gets into the inside of your glass the salt will ruin the flavor balance you are building between sweet and salty. Place it back in the freezer to firm up your rim garnish

Second, in your shaker place juice of one key lime and 2 oz. of tequila (tequila is the second way you are using the agave plant - see tequila's interesting history under the margarita recipe).

Third, put in a handful of ice and shake 10 times.

Fourth, pour into your frosted glass and alternate with the blood orange soda until full. Enjoy!

GRAPEFRUIT DAZY | serves 2

3 - 1.5 oz. Tequila blanca
1.5 oz. Orange liqueur
1.5 oz. Lime juice + sliced lime wheel
1.5 oz. Fresh grapefruit juice
Ice
Chili salt (recipe follows)

First, rim your glass with lime juice and dip into chili salt mixture. This is simply taking cayenne pepper and mixing it with salt. Place garnished glass in your freezer to frost for 1 to 2 minutes.

Second, add ingredients to shaker with ice and shake vigorously for a count of 10.

Third, strain into your frosted and salted glass and garnish with two thin lime wheels to enjoy.

HOW OTHER PARENTS DO IT:

When Should You Feed Them?

"I have three kids all about four years apart. And I have run the gamut from being a helicopter-parent to 'BUT-DID-YOU-DIE?' style. Especially after having my third child who is seven and three-quarter years old. It's amazing and freeing to be the 'BUT-DID-YOU-DIE' kind. If they fall, I say – 'What a great fall.' If they put dirt in their mouth I wonder if they even need dinner. Try it for a season. You'll thank me."
-Yolanda, Santa Fe, NM

This page has been left blank for your planning or notes)

CHAPTER 6: NUCLEATING NINES AND THE TEMERARIOUS TENS

"I could say that I let my kids play unsupervised because I want to foster independence, but I yell less when I have no idea what is happening." -Momonymous

While your nine-year-old restructures their identity and you notice that your ten-year-old makes reckless mistakes let's sit down and talk about:

- Raging tempers
- Not having fear in love
- The control façade
- How to embrace chaos

Later we will sit down with a nice Strawberry Chamomile, French Pear Martini, or an Irish Maid to soothe our souls.

Ahh, the start of the tween years. Kill you in public and love you in private, it is like dating the worst person ever.

This stage is fraught with transition, transition, transition, and a lot of awkwardness. They crave independence and time away from parents, but they still really need us and want us. Even if they do not want to hold hands in public or cuddle as much, they still desire parental attention. They start to strongly want to be a part of making family decisions, big and small.

The difficult part of parenting this age is letting go of the idea that you are in control.

I recently was rereading <u>Loving Your Kids on Purpose</u> by Danny Silk and found this nugget of parenting truth. Our beliefs determine our interpretation of events. Those interpretations dictate our feelings and prepare us to act in a way consistent with our own beliefs. The lie is we believe that we can control others. When an adult can't get a child to do what he or she wants or to stop doing what she doesn't want, the adult often introduces the dynamic of violence into the relationship to gain control of the child. This can be done with angry voices, corporal punishment, throwing items around the house, or slamming doors in frustration.

When my beautiful, sweet kids screw up, my go-to reaction was, If I control them; I will feel like I have some control over the quality in my own life.

I remember sitting in a moms meeting talking to a reserved mom who on top of being a scientist had twice the number of children I had. She never seemed to "lose it". If anyone was going to know exactly what to do, it had to be her. When I was finally able to broach the subject of control, her contrite answer was, "I don't know, I just don't. I control myself".

I could feel the boil of anger start in my belly as soon as her paltry answer left her mouth and entered my ears.

When it reached my chest, I felt myself screaming in my head "BUT HOW??!! HOW DO YOU CONTROL YOURSELF!" Frantically, I tried to reel in my rage, put my party face back on… which is far easier with someone you are not in charge of how they turn out as adults… and dropped the subject altogether.

Somewhere in a mix of chagrin and rage, I knew that to get to the bottom of this, I was going to have to reveal the ugly truth about myself.

I lost my temper way more than I should have with my kids. I couldn't yet control myself.

I realize now WAAAAAAAAAYYYYYYYY afterward (but it stills feels like the realization dawned just yesterday), that I needed to get real with why I was angry. That took me a long and windy way of self-discovery, painful authenticity, and self-care.

I felt out-of-control. I felt others could control me. I was afraid of what it would mean if I let that control go. I needed to control time, but these precious growing kids don't want to be controlled.

I swear G-d must have really wanted me to learn this lesson because He sent me exactly who I needed, TWO OF THEM. Three, if you count my husband. Three beings who will not be controlled. They helped me on this journey to figuring out the big fat reason why I was angry.

My life up until that point of understanding felt controlled by emotions, people, and situations.

My family's lack of falling in-line made me feel out of control. I tried to break this learned pattern, teaching myself that no one is responsible for me but me. That no one can make me feel or behave in any way. I get to determine my own destiny. With that realization, it was like a switch was flipped on. I gained this ability to calm down in situations where I felt out of control and think of myself as a mirror reflecting instead of absorbing and imploding and then subsequently exploding, Mount Vesuvius style.

I have had my children tell me they can remember the moment my parenting changed. Recently, my own mother, eight years after my kids had told me, commented something similar. "Why are you different? What have you done to change yourself? Where can I get some?" Finally, all the self-work I have done has bled over into other relationships of my life.

The painful truth I had to realize is that there is no fear in love.

NO FEAR IN LOVE.

Does this mean that I stopped being angry? Hell no. For years I thought that being angry was a "sin". Like something was wrong with me, I was somehow doing life & motherhood wrong. I am here to tell you guys that there is nothing wrong with being angry. There is only "sin" in what you do in anger. Anger is the tool to let you know that there is a problem that needs reflection.

I had to learn tools to deal with my pot of boiling anger. Just like with cooking, when my pot begins to boil, I have to take the lid off and let the building pressure of steam out.

In the beginning, I needed to environmentally remove myself. Later, I learned to say, "I am going to need a minute to think" and then walk away to do just that. I also hold my breath in my cheeks and slowly let it out. I learned that there is no rush to speak or solve anything. Once you're past parenting the six-year-old age, your discipline doesn't need to be immediate.

Oddly, this is also the time that kids really can push your buttons emotionally. They have learned what makes you tick. That is the core job of being a kid, push to figure out where the lines are. More than ever it is okay to take the time and reflect before speaking.

It is very easy as a parent to give away your self-control to the mistake of the child. Our thinking turns off and our emotions go into overdrive. We need to breathe deep before we speak to reduce and process our own fear and anxiety instead of generating and misplacing it.

My mantra for this stage of parenting is that "no one can control us, and we can't control others".

CONTROL IS A FAÇADE.

Have you ever seen a sped up slow-motion flower blooming video? Those are my parenting fists. It seems that every day I am learning to unclench my control fists a little more. Each moment of parenting has brought a lesson where I learn that I am being tight-fisted about something, some idea, some notion and I am obliged to figure out how to unclench and release that control.

I am starting to think that coming to the twilight years of my parenting that it was all about me. These kids came into my life, wrecked it, turned it in on itself to teach me that I have never been in control of anything.

Alison Gopnik, a child developmental psychologist, wrote a book in 2017 titled, The Gardener and the Carpenter. She takes a hard look at the culture around "parenting". Apparently, this is a new invention from the seventies, thinking that it is something we do, something we have control over. Like a carpenter, using the right plans and tools, we will have control over how our kids turn out. Ergo, if they turn out "wrong" (not the way you had intended) the blame fell on your shoulders. You should have done something differently.

I have had the displeasure of experiencing the weight of this realization and thought process and I have seen my friends crushed under their personal weight of parent-guilt as well.

Gopnik, like John Taylor Gatto, who wrote the Underground History of American Education, considers that our twenty-first century "facts" of how children learn, and how we should parent are based on bad science. That we have become intensely obsessive, controlling, and a goal-oriented labor force trying in vain to create a particular kind of child who becomes a particular kind of adult.

HOW THEN SHOULD WE PARENT?

I love when Gopnik compares what we should be doing as parents to gardeners. I don't see it as some "cutting-edge-science" but more of a return to our ancestral ways. Kids, like life, are messy and unpredictable.

If we were to plant a garden, we plant hopes and wishes that it will grow and flourish. However, we don't have control over other environmental factors that will be introduced to our gardens planted out in the world. The weather, soil, and the occasional cat that stealthily climbs in looking all cute and innocent to take and bury a crap will have an effect on what grows and how it turns out.

We do not parent in a vacuum. Our children are out in the world, some more than others. Try as you might you cannot create a perfect experiment to test out raising kids. There are no control groups only mass amounts of variables that create a beautiful chaos in our lives.

EMBRACING CHAOS

Life is predictable in that it is unpredictable. It will throw you opportunity after opportunity to learn to adapt and improvise, developing our resiliency.

For me, this is the essence of what I am learning in being a parent. I cannot force order and perfection from myself. I cannot fill myself up with regretful poison looking back at past choices I made and trying to carry the blame of why my kids do what they do because of me. To exist is to survive unfair choices at some point. And in parenting, there are so many paths we could take, but ultimately, we have to take one.

The pain of hindsight is that it makes it seem easy to look back and say, well clearly that was the wrong one and that one was the right one. However, there is no right path. There is what you took and the consequences of those choices both good and different.

If you can, try to realize this early on in your parenting adventure, you are not on a deserted island "gardening" a life for your family alone. There are other family members with you who will affect how things occur. There are your kids whose responses change with their growth. There are the "cats who anonymously stop to poop" in yours and your kid's life-garden – that is something you don't always see but will inevitably affect how your garden grows.

Who the f**k knows how it is all going to actually turn out. You have to make a choice and run with it. Leave the anxiety behind, it is crippling you. Make a choice, learn from it and change when needed. Life is constantly changing with you.

This page has been left blank for your planning or notes

STRAWBERRY CHAMOMILE
Carrytail | Shake | Coupe Glass | 1 serving
How I managed to keep the kids alive but kill every houseplant I have ever owned is beyond me!

INGREDIENTS
1 oz. Elderflower cordial
1 Tbsp. Sliced fresh ginger
0.5 oz. Simple syrup *(see pg. 30 for directions)*
4 oz. Chamomile tea
2 Strawberries
5 Mint leaves + top sprig for garnish
Ice
Orange and lemon wheel to garnish

STEP 1
Muddle *(see pg. 30 for directions)* together strawberries, ginger, mint, and syrup with the handle of a wooden spoon in a shaker.

STEP 2
Add the rest of the ingredients and ice. Shake for a count of 10.

STEP 3
Fine strain into a frosted glass. Garnish with the mint sprig and the orange and lemon wheel slices to enjoy!

This drink is easy to switch up with whatever berry is in season.

This page has been left blank for your planning or notes

FRENCH PEAR MARTINI
Cocktail | Shake | Martini Glass | 1 serving
Great parenting lies in the middle of "DON'T DO THAT!" and "Oh, what the hell."

INGREDIENTS
1.5 oz. Elderflower liqueur
1.5 oz. Vodka
2 oz. Pear juice + thin slice of a pear for garnish
Lemon slice for garnishing the sugar
White baking sugar
Ice

STEP 1
Rub the rim of your glass with a cut lemon and then coat with sugar. Place in your freezer to frost while you make the rest of your drink.

STEP 2
Place all ingredients into your shaker with ice and shake vigorously for a count of 10.

STEP 3
Strain into your frosted rimmed glass and enjoy. Garnish with a thin slice of pear. Enjoy!

(This page has been left blank for your planning or notes)

IRISH MAID
Cocktail | Shake | Rocks Glass | 1 serving
Cleaning house with kids is like brushing your teeth while eating Oreos.

INGREDIENTS
2 Slices quarter-inch thick cucumber wheels + extra for garnish
2 oz. Irish single malt whiskey
0.5 oz. St. Germaine
0.75 oz. Lemon juice
0.75 oz. Simple syrup *(see pg. 30 for directions)*
Ice

STEP 1
Muddle *(see pg. 30 for directions)* cucumber at the bottom of your shaker with a wooden spoon handle.

STEP 2
Add the remaining ingredients with ice and shake vigorously for a count of 10.

STEP 3
Strain into your frosted glass and garnish with a two to three thin cucumber slices, enjoy!

HOW OTHER PARENTS DO IT:

If You Want It – Work For It.

"I have realized that my kid only speaks in black and white. He understands things that are measurable. Realizing that I fly off the handle when I am angry, I have a system in place for things they want, like WIFI; and things I want, like a clean kitchen, bathroom, and a straight house.

It is exhausting to change the WIFI password every day, but I yell and say things less like 'your ass is grass, and I am the lawnmower.' Now when they need to be grounded, I don't turn into Beast from Beauty and the Beast when he yells 'Then go ahead and STARVVVVEEE!'

I have an ingenious chart I keep close by that has specific things they can do which determines how long the grounding lasts. I love it because it takes me out of the position of being the furious judge who vacillates from eternity to a couple of hours.

The way it works: I figure out what the appropriate amount of points correlating to what they did to get in trouble. I keep a list of to do's that I feel suit what I am trying to teach the kids, serve others and then I put points beside the items that they can choose what they want to earn to work their way out of grounding. I have only been using this for six months, so it might come back to bite me in the ass. Hey, it is working for now. When there is a new problem, I'll figure out a new solution."

Denis - dad of one, Anchorage, AK

Congratulations! You Have Found Yourself Grounded. Earn X Points to End Your Sentence.

CHARITY WORK	POINTS	CHARITY WORK	POINTS	CHARITY WORK	POINTS	CHARITY WORK	POINTS
Wash the dog		Clean the blinds		Pick up the litter at a park		Pick an organization to volunteer for and do it	
Clean out the microwave		Clean out the refrigerator		Clean all the toilets in the house		Chores for an elderly neighbor	
Pick up dog poop		Hold doors for others in public		Write your grandparents a nice letter			
Sweep cobwebs off walls and porch		Wash, dry, and fold family member's laundry		Make dinner for the family			
Sweep garage		Make special dessert for sibling		Ask your aunt or uncle how you can help			
Clean the base molding		Organize the garage		Make beds for the family for 3 mornings			

CHAPTER 7: EDACIOUS ELEVENS AND THE TETCHY TWELVES

"Fun parenting drinking game: take a shot every time your child whines. Just kidding, don't do this, you'll die." —Dadonymous

In the years that you have a consuming eleven-year-old and a suddenly bad-tempered twelve-year-old, you will be covered because you have read this chapter that is all about:

- Idle hands and the devil's workshop – figuring out when to push
- Cultivating motivation
- Gardening vs. Carpentry

I know they can make you cray cray but let me top you off with a 3 Kids in a Cup, Lavender Lemonade (+ 3 variations to boot!), or decadence in a cup called Emerald Spice.

IDLE HANDS

We have had a societal pendulum swing to an incredibly involved parenting style and overscheduling our kids. The driving force is the concern that boredom is the gateway to drugs and rebellion. Dr. Caldwell has conducted a lot of research on "leisure studies" at Penn State and has found that it isn't just kids with free time who are bored. Really busy kids just as easily get bored. Revealing that the problem isn't a boredom problem at all but an intrinsic motivation problem.

Allow me to firm up this mushy explanation. The road to kids figuring themselves out and learning to make better decisions doesn't come from having too much free time, or a full schedule with little to no rope to hang themselves. It comes from not having the practice of self-examination.

Having too much free time or being super busy correlates to poor decisions, but the cause of these decisions has more to do with where a teen's brain is in development. Neuroscientist Dr. Galvan at UCLA has shown that during the teen years the part of the brain responsible for weighing risk and consequences is hijacked by the pleasure area. Asking teens, "Didn't you see that was a bad idea?!" isn't even a reasonable question. Yes, in an abstract setting they can see the fallacy in the decisions of others, but in the real-life-excitement-of-the-moment, they can't.

IS IT ALL IN VAIN?

No, don't lose hope. There are two keys, give your kids opportunities to examine what is going on internally, and to motivate themselves.

Help them get in the habit of asking themselves, "Am I bored in general or is the situation boring? Am I doing this because I want to or are my friends/family making me?" These self-reflection questions build a habit of critical conscious thinking.

Not having idle hands is not an unhealthy idea. What is a bad idea is not knowing how to entertain yourself? If your kids grow used to you always filling their free time, then they will be poorly prepared to motivate themselves to become the architects of their own time. Having the free time alone to figure out for yourself how to counteract situational boredom is part of healthy development. Having the ability to make choices about what activities and interests you want to pursue (meaning, not having mom or dad choose it for you) is equally important to your child's development and veering a little further away from poor choices; though not to misguide you, this it is not a cure-all.

There is, of course, a caveat. If you find your child can not entertain themselves and are up underneath you ALL THE TIME or seeking out other adults, even strangers to entertain them… they are crying out for your attention. Time to stop and take a hard look at how much quality time you are spending with them. They are giving you a giant-smack-you-in-the-face clue that they need you.

MY STRUGGLE

For our family, it was exactly around this age that we needed a change. My grandma who lived on a small farm and never took a day off was fond of saying "Idle hands are the devil's workshop". She especially liked to say it chastising me for sleeping in until six in the morning when I would visit. Short of having a farm to raise my kiddos, there is only so much housework a homeschooling kid can or should do before Child Protective Services might need to be called.

Enter activities. We signed up for everything. My kids have always had vast interests and desires to learn and try anything. Our hands were kept busy with music, art, and sports.

However, just for fun, my kids would time a dramatic performance at the first of every practice; replete with dragging a kid to a begged activity. I don't know what happens but somewhere from the time we ask them what they want to sign up for, until the first day, they, unbeknownst to me, decide they can't or won't do it.

What am I to do with a crying-yelling-door-locking kid?

I have one special memory when it was my first time to parent out-of-state: away from my parents and in-laws. We'd moved to Alaska, along with no longer having my physical support system I was now learning to deal with the harshest winters I had ever experienced. I had to part drag and part push my 12-year-old up a slippery iced-over sidewalk to her figure skating practice. Something she has previously loved for the last four years. However, in this moment, she is too afraid to go in after begging me to find her a great coach. Her excitement of going vanished from her memory as we drove up. I tried talking, understanding, love, and support; she was having none of it. We must have looked like a vaudeville-sight slipping up the sidewalk. The entrance had two doors to enter, called a winter entrance, she actually sat down in-between them and said "No, mom. I can't. I don't want to. I hate you for forcing me."

...What? In the holy hell? You asked me to sign you up?!...

"Well, that is too bad. Because I love you, and you are going." She had pushed my resolve. That was it, I was determined to get her into what I had paid for. We were ten minutes late, but we were inside and putting on her skates. Even up to the point of getting on the ice she was seething through gritted teeth, "No", I told her, "You have to at least try this practice. Now go. You. Can. Do. It!"

Many parenting books will tell you "how to talk" to your kids, "how to help" them; but damn, does anyone have as hard-headed kids as me? When and for how long am I supposed to push? In what situations? Is all this forcing doing more damage than good?

At this point in my parenting walk, I had learned to be gentle with my words. I was desperately working on not answering foolish behavior with more foolishness. I have to be honest with you, in the heat of the moment, kids can make you question your sanity.

This age and example are not like a "naughty chair" timeout from that show "The Nanny" that will be able to help; this is a child who is almost your size.

"Are you really doing the right thing?" was on repeat over and over in my head. "When do you force? Do you even force?" My brain was inundated with self-doubt, but I forged ahead with action. Something deeply internal told me to keep going.

Finally, my daughter gets out on the ice and is smiling (not at me, of course) within five minutes. 55 more minutes to go; I decided to call my dad.

I poured my heart out to him.

"Listen, honey. You never really know until the end. And there's never an end to parenting. What I can tell you is that I think you did do the right thing today and pushed her. Sometimes they need a push to do great things. The only thing that helped me decide if it was time to push you guys was to ask myself, 'If it was good for your physical, mental, spiritual health?' If I could say 'yes' to those questions, then I pushed, but only for what and how long we had signed you guys up for. Go ahead and push her until you are finished with the lessons you have purchased, then let her decide if she wants to continue."

Thank G-d for telephones and parents.

After my phone-a-wiser-parent-call, I went back in to watch her practice and keep my younger one busy. When she was finished, she came off the ice and hugged me. She said, (I am not kidding...) "Thank you for making me, mom! I had the best time, and I made a new friend!"

I still have PTSD from these years.

Whippersnappers forget the battle completely, but for us, that sh*t lingers. These days, I am firmer in my resolve in what my father taught me during that phone call. Push them if it is for their betterment.

OBDURATE YOUTHS

Now, the gritty truth is that there are some years kids are stubborn and won't want to sign up for anything. I have had to develop a new addendum "You have to do something. Either you choose, or I will."

It never goes over easy. However, reminding them that they can either have autonomy in their choice or not is enough to motivate them to choose an activity. Each and every time (apart from once), they were better for it.

We had just finished traveling for several months when my husband and I noticed that our youngest was really struggling with not having a purpose. It was bleeding over into him, becoming a social recluse and gaming seemed to be his sole interest. We don't have strong opinions on video-gaming or computer usage, we find there are several positives to them as tools. We do, however, have very strong opinions on being singular in your interests, especially at such a young age. So, when we moved into our current home, we knew that he needed to choose something. It did not go over well. He refused to choose. We suggested past interests, wrestling, scouts, art but to no avail. I am not sure how Jiu-Jitsu first came about, but my husband decided that he wanted to start taking classes and asked our son to join him. We argued over dinner, which is always pleasant. Our son had his point of view, we had ours; finally, an agreement was reached. He would try a couple of classes, but if he didn't like it that would be the end of it, and we'd continue the search for something else. That was a year and a half ago as of the writing of this paragraph. He has gone on to a revolving door pursuing many other activities and interests, but Jiu-Jitsu remains to be his thing. Fortunately, for our travel-loving-selves, we attend the Barra family gyms and can attend any class at any Barra gym around the world.

The time that it did backfire was a government class taught by a lawyer that I pushed for because our oldest studies law on her own time for fun. Knowing what I now know about how important it is for them to choose for themselves I can see how it blew up. When my oldest finished the semester, we both agreed that it was horrible-no-good-decision. But hey, there is always a silver lining; we ~~argued~~ communicated, and we learned more of what our boundaries were.

CULTIVATING MOTIVATION

When the kids are little, the easiest way to ~~manipulate~~ motivate them is using the "carrot – stick" model. If you do this, you get a sweet little reward or this painful punishment. What happens when you have a kid who could not care less about the reward or the punishment?

Over the years, I have had several friends who have had kids who did not respond at all to having things taken away. Even if it was everything, electronics, friend time, their bedroom door, their bed, their entire wardrobe. These same kids gave the same amount of care when they were rewarded, no matter how sweet the reward, they did not and would not perform. Complete apathy.

I always felt truly bad for these friends, but not until my oldest started to act the same way was I able to sympathize with how daunting it can be to parent a child who will not be motivated.

WHAT WAS MISSING?

Sometimes, if you are open to it, the help can come from the unlikeliest places. I was attending a business conference when someone mentioned Dan Pink's TED talk on "The Puzzle of Motivation". He talked about what companies need to do to better motivate their employees' productivity. I watched it and was blown away by how applicable it was to parenting.

The "carrot – stick" method works when you are establishing a simple set of rules with a clear destination. This is because rewards will narrow our focus and concentrate our minds. When you want your kid to stop peeing their pants, make healthy eating choices, keep their room straight, get good grades this is usually a great method to have in your toolbox.

When that isn't working, realize the problem does not always lie with your unmotivated a**hole of a kid who is keeping you up at night with worries of their bleak future. You might need to create an environment for you to overcome your functional fixedness. Incentivization is killing your family's creativity and stagnating your thinking about how to overcome.

When you are approaching teen-ness (and most white-collar jobs) there is no clear set of rules with an obvious solution. There are mystifying problems with unobvious solutions. If you want your apathetic kid to engage, they are probably going to need more opportunity with self-direction. The longer we exist in life the more cognitive skill is needed to navigate it.

GREAT. NOW, WHAT DO WE DO INSTEAD?

I don't know.

Therein lies the freedom to try. Now that I look back on my eldest's messiness of apathy I can see it for what it was, a beginning. She was letting us know that we needed to try something new. Part of the way out of the mess you feel when you are parenting a mystifying kid is that you must keep trying new and uncomfortable things.

What we started trying was letting go. My husband and I sat down and discussed what were the handful of things we needed rules for, we established our clear boundaries with her as parents and then let go. We asked her to think for herself. These long late-night talks and heated discussions started to happen. She'd tentatively bring problems to us, slowly trusting that there wouldn't be punitive measures and we'd ask her what she thought needed to be done. Over time it seemed like she began to really think things through. She began to realize that sometimes temptation is high, and motivation can be low. She started setting boundaries for herself that required more Environmental Engineering so that she didn't have to wait for motivation to show up or rely on her own willpower to overcome.

I don't want to paint a portrait of perfection, the girl still messed up. I won't lie, it was incredibly difficult to not tell her what we thought she should do, because we TOTALLY knew how to easily fix it. What we came to cherish was that she was open enough to bring all her garbage to the table and sort through it with us, finding her own way to a solution. When she started bringing her friends to "talk" with us about their devastatingly secret problems, we saw that we had unintentionally stumbled onto something special.

"So, awesome. Now you have your kid and other kids telling you their problems, what does that actually fix? How does that help them?"

In this century, "left-brain" tasks are becoming easy to outsource and automate, job descriptions are changing and requiring us to do more creative wayfinding in problem-solving. I think, that as parents of this century's kids, we need to prepare them for this new world approach. Developing more intrinsic motivation with building blocks of autonomy and purpose; shifting away from the reward model and moving towards letting them learn not just what choices to make but how to make them.

I get it, most of us would prefer if parenting was less ambiguous, more like carpentry. We choose the life and child we want, follow the instructions for measuring and cutting, then voila! You have finished a project. The problem is parenting is more like gardening than carpentry. Meaning, despite all your tender care there are outside influences affecting the development; it is partially up to the plant to also defend itself and become resourceful.

If we are always making the decisions for our children as they grow up, they fail to learn how to make choices and become equipped to deal with the ever-new situations life will throw us in to. What would change if we started telling our kids, "You don't get a reward for your behavior, you get to figure out your problem; let's see what happens. I'll be here if you need me"?

This page has been left blank for your planning or notes

THREE KIDS IN A CUP
Cocktail | Shake | Jam Jar | 1 serving

As kids, we wondered why our parents were always in a bad mood now, we are like … oooooooooh.

INGREDIENTS
1 oz. Vodka
1 oz. Tequila blanca
0.5 oz. Lime juice
0.75 oz. Fresh grapefruit juice
0.5 oz. Simple syrup *(see pg. 30 for directions)*
1 tsp. Maraschino liquor
2 dashes Angostura bitters
Ice
Orange peel
Fine strainer

STEP 1
Shake all ingredients with ice in your shaker for a count of 10.

STEP 2
Fine strain into your frosted glass and garnish with an orange peel. Enjoy!

(This page has been left
blank for your planning
or notes)

LAVENDER LEMONADE

Carrytail | Shake | Highball Glass | 1 serving

I don't know about you, but I have thought about running away more as an adult than I ever did as a child.

INGREDIENTS

½ oz. Lavender syrup *(see pg. 20 for directions)*
6 oz. Lemonade
Ice
Purple flower blossom like lavender for garnish
Sliced lemon wheel

STEP 1

Add ingredients to shaker with ice and shake vigorously for a count of 10.

STEP 2

Fine strain into a frosted glass. Garnish with a lemon wheel and a purple flower blossom, like a lavender bloom. Serve and enjoy!

VARIATION:

Add 2 oz of pineapple juice, it darkens the color and adds a nice layer of complexity to the drink.

COCKTAIL VARIATIONS:

You can go simple and just add 1.5 oz. of whisk(e)y, bourbon, or gin. If you want to get a little fancier see the two variations below.

MEDINA RIVER

Build this drink in your frosted glass. First, add 1.5 oz. of whisk(e)y and 1 oz. shot of Cointreau then stir in lavender syrup and lemonade.

The Medina river is one of my favorite spots to float with family and friends. The water is gentle, crystal clear and just like this drink, perfect for the blistering hot days of summer here in Texas.

LAVENDER BRAMBLE

Add 1.5 oz. gin and 0.5 oz. Cream de Cassis to your lavender lemonade ingredients in your shaker. Shake for a count of 10 and fine strain into your frosted glass.

This page has been left blank for your planning or notes

EMERALD SPICE

Cocktail | Shake | Coupe Glass | 2 servings

Why do they want dinner every single night, breakfast every single morning, and lunch?!

INGREDIENTS
4 - 1.5 oz. Shots of gin
4 tsps. Sugar
1 oz. Lemon or lime juice
8 Slices of ginger
10 Green peppercorns
4 Basil leaves
Ice

STEP 1
Muddle *(see pg. 30 for directions)* with the handle of a wooden spoon sugar, ginger, basil, lemon, peppercorns at the bottom of your shaker until the sugar is dissolved.

STEP 2
Add the gin and ice and shake vigorously for a count of 15.

STEP 3
Divide and strain into two frosted glasses. Garnish each with a slice of candied ginger. Enjoy!

We fell in love with fresh green peppercorns while living in Thailand. These can be tricky to find in the U.S. I have had good luck finding jarred green peppercorns in Asian groceries, or Amazon. Make sure to rinse their brine off before using.
If you can't find green, use pink peppercorns instead - totally different flavor but still great.

HOW OTHER PARENTS DO IT:

Pick Your Battles Wisely.

"My son and I were home alone while my wife and two daughters were out shopping. I had decided I was going to go all out and make a special father-son lunch. Triston had decided about a minute before we sat down to eat that he no longer liked broccoli. That he, in fact, had never liked broccoli in all his eleven years of life. So, when I called him to eat with me, he immediately informed me of MY forgetful error.

My thought process went as follows:
1. I cooked it.
2. He is going to eat it.
3. Even if it kills me. Because really, it IS my job to make him become a functioning member of society.
4. ... & the starving children everywhere.

We got as far as one bite. That piece of broccoli stayed in his mouth for 2.5 hours. When his mother arrived home; she looked between the two of us. Asked Triston how he was, and with his right cheek puffed out like a chipmunk he whimpered 'I hate broccoli and I don't want to eat it.' To which she turned and asked me to join her in the pantry.

'How long have you been fighting this battle, my brave king?'
'Two and a half hours.'
We locked eyes and entered a staring game.
... ... *I blinked.*
'Well, who do you think is really winning here?' She says *somehow still not blinking.*

There are many battles that a parent fights while raising tiny humans to become polite productive members of society. Apparently, you cannot fight them all. Also, my kid can hold a piece of broccoli in his mouth for TWO AND HALF HOURS!

What I have learned is, to never pick food as a battle in our home again (and I need to work on my staring game)."
-Mike - dad of three, Austin, TX.

This page has been left blank for your planning or notes

CHAPTER 8: TENUOUS THIRTEENS AND THE FRAGILE FOURTEENS

"Before becoming a parent, I didn't know I could ruin someone's life by asking them to put on longer shorts." -Dadonymous

Before you start dealing with doubtful thirteen-year-olds and easily broken fourteen-year-olds read this chapter on:

- Don't tell them they're…
- The science behind praise
- The next level of learning: apprenticeships

And for the love of yourself make sure you imbibe with a Mexican Martini, Cucumber Collins (plus all the variations), and a delightful Primavera (and its variation)

DON'T TELL YOUR KID THEY ARE SMART ...*but don't tell them they are dumb either...*

Columbia University has told us that 85% of us parents think that we should naturally tell our kid he is smart, but science tells us "nope". You are just making it worse if you do.

I am so glad I read this study AFTER I had raised one child and have 5 years left with the second one.

The first kid is so smart that if she can't do something perfectly right away, she has the tendency to quit. Makes sense, right? How the hell did that happen? For years I was certain that the genesis for this zero-tolerance policy of hers came from that third-grade science fair project where I was on her to write neat, cut neat, and glue neat. Even though she won first place, that pressure had obviously made her afraid. I realize that sounds like I am saying, my insistence for gluing paper to cardboard correctly is what helped her win and subsequently develop a neurosis. At the time, I was more certain of the latter than the former.

HOW I CAME TO THIS CONCLUSION

I began to notice her become frozen with perfection. I had placed high standards on her ...*I realized they were high after looking at the other kids' work...* I went to the internet to find my echo chamber on how demanding parents create anxious children. I didn't have time to bother with finding actual valid research to back this idea up. I just knew that if I could find statements confirming what I had already believed about my self-loathing self, it was virtually a fact. No need to dig further.

I radically changed my parenting as a reaction. I laxed on perfection embraced living in the mess and chaos.

Nothing changed. If anything, it became worse.

THE OTHER LAYER

To my chagrin, it was years later that I read Dweck's [actual-real-science-with-a-multitude-of-case-studies] research on why brilliant girls become tenuous. Within those intrusive findings, I felt like she and her team must have had surveillance on our family.

Between each pendulum swing of my parenting styles, perfection to chaos, I had opened Pandora's box of praise. I kept telling my kid that she was "so smart/brilliant/wonderful/genius". She could do anything. I particularly remember making sure that she heard it because all I heard my friends and family say to her was "Wow! She is extraordinarily beautiful." No way was I going to raise a daughter who thought she was only as good as her looks. *Viva la revolution! Strong, intelligent, independent, just like Beyoncé had told me.*

Oops.

Research has shown us that if you praise a kid for their effort, "you work really hard.", it gives them a variable they can control. Elements we can control are what we find the easiest to trust because we like to be in control.

"They" did a test where kids praised simply by one line, "you're smart" or "you work hard". Invariably and with shocking results, the "work hard" praise got the kids to do well and even try harder for the next go around.

Dweck designed and administered a test crafted to make kids fail with the intention of seeing the effect of two different types of praise, generic and specific. If kids were given specific praise, "You worked really hard on that.", scored 30% higher on a subsequent test. Freaking 30 percent higher.

Students who were given the generic praise like, "It's ok, I know you're really smart.", failed each time. Worse yet, 20% of them didn't even try the next time.

WHY?

It's been found that the smart kids who were given generic praise assumed that the failure meant that the jig is up. They really aren't smart; why even try?

WHAT TO DO INSTEAD?

Your praise must be specific and authentic. It is too easy to say, "You did great!" I know that it sounds corny and it definitely takes much longer to say but try, "I really like that you keep trying even if it is hard".

There are a ton more studies that you can read by Dweck and Baumeister. Interestingly, Baumeister set out to disprove Dweck's original findings but since replicating the data with his own experiments has become a convert.

We, as parents, think we are being supportive. Especially when we see them struggling. We want to reach out and say, "You can do it! I know you can. You are so smart.", your kid, however, is calling bullsh*t. There is nothing in that type of praise that he can use to measure himself. Vacuous over-praise ruins their self-esteem and primes them to burden themselves with a pressure ready to erupt like a long overdue volcano. Over time this causes them to become little narcissistic a**holes with a growing interest in tearing others down. I am not being dramatic; if anything, I am understating.

BACK OFF AND LIGHTLY PEPPER IN SPECIFIC PRAISE.

As I said before, I read this research after one child was a baby adult and the other was in their early teen years. What makes this particular parenting faux pau so difficult to own up to is that before having my kids I was a teacher. I knew that specific praise was more valuable than generic. Somewhere in becoming a parent all of that got lost in translation. It just did not feel natural to do it with my own babies. Unfortunately, I can see that this was a grave mistake as plain as the nose on my face.

WHEN YOU KNOW BETTER, DO BETTER.

I have corrected myself and made this above statement my meditation mantra that I take to heart. Interestingly, if it takes to tear down old habits, my reinforcement comes through the quickness with which I see changes in my kids. No lie, the confidence with which I see them take on difficult tasks has greatly improved and brings tears to my eyes.

Earlier on in this book I wrote about two methods to help kids from babies and twelve learn best, now that you have teenagers there is a third and final layer of learning that you need to introduce.

This is the perfect age that learns best by apprenticeship.

Apprenticeships are a method of learning where they work with a master at a skill, gaining a valuable experience that would not otherwise be gained. From this, they develop a deeper belief and confidence in their ability to do something. When we go through this type of training and achieve a skill, we internalize that we really can "do it" giving us the confidence to continue to try and learn in life.

All those friends and community that you have spent a lifetime cultivating are the ones you draw from now to see how to connect your teen to someone who they can have a short apprenticeship under. This process is what will build upon the budding autonomy they need to have in themselves to take on adulthood.

While they were babies you were building the bridge of connection by showing them that communication was important, setting a foundation of trust, that when they need to, they can come to you and talk because you will listen to them. Then as littles, you taught them the freedom of self-independence, letting them learn by doing by themselves. Now is the time you are putting on the finishing touches of who they are before they stumble into adulting. You start this by letting them gain skills that can help them grow a true belief in themselves that they can do and learn. An apprenticeship is unique in instruction because they have a master showing them that they are also helping as they have grown in knowledge.

These skills of all sorts be it cooking, building, investing, or creating, teach that we are adroit with our minds and hands and that is what we need to become successful in life. You are raising children who need to be strong enough to stand alone, smart enough to know when they need help, and brave enough to ask for it. This must be built into them over time, you cannot just tell it to them and expect them to internalize it. There are steps and a process to help weave it into the fabric of their being. That is why these three key phases of learning, talking, doing, and apprenticeships are integral and achieve more than anything you try to tell or praise in your kid's attempts.

FURTHER CONFIRMATION…AS IF YOU NEEDED IT

This Dr. Ng, a scholar at the university of Illinois, – set up a heinous test, but the findings are consistent with the inverse truth of empty praise and ignoring-the-elephant-in-the-room style of parenting.

The kids were given a test that induced a sense of failure. In the middle of the test, the kids would be given a five-minute break where they could go see their moms. However, before the moms went in to see their children, they (the moms) were lied to. They were told the raw score of their child but then told it was a significantly below average score. I know, I said it was a heinous test.

THE FINDINGS

U.S. moms remained upbeat during the five-minute interval with their child. Despite being told that their child was a complete and utter failure AND that there was a possibility that this failure might need to go on their permanent record, the parents never brought up the test or scores in conversation. Instead, the U.S. moms talked about everything and anything but the problematic test. Interestingly, Chinese moms came in and said "You are not concentrating hard enough. Let's look at the problems on the test and see what we can do about it."

Before everyone nods complacently and thinks, "well, obviously. Tiger moms", it is worth noting that both sets of mothers were equally demonstrative in showing love, affection, and smiles.

When the kids go back in to finish the test, that has been designed to make them fail, the Chinese kids end up scoring 33% better than their American counterparts! What does that tell us? Demands don't break the child. Caging the elephant in the room and immeasurable praises do.

A NOTE FOR MYSELF & OTHER PRAISE JUNKIES

If we don't let our kids struggle, their brains fail to develop a strong capacity knowing they have the ability to work through a frustrating spell. As hard as it is, we need to let them flounder, fail, cry.

This is not abandoning them to the wolves. We still get to be in their corners as their personal cheerleader. Changing our cheer to, "I am so proud you keep trying! I love that you work hard, even when it is not easy." When they are involved in learning some set of skills this gives us something useful to point to when praising them. You can fake or cheat a skill. You either have it or not. When you see your kids working through tough spots you can tell them, "Hey. I see you, and I like that you are working hard to learn."

I am adding this paragraph in well after I have finished writing this book. At this moment in my life my nephew, his wife and two little babies (five & two) have moved in with us. I have gotten so used to using specific praise that I do it without thinking. My five-year-old grandnephew initially during the first few days was telling me how great I was at whatever I was doing, after his first week of being here things shifted and I heard him start repeating my own praises back to me. Usually, I have some creative project to work on in the evenings as a way to unwind, I was working on a "difficult to me" cross-stitch pattern and he came up to me and said, "Auntcole, I really like how you keep working even when it is hard for you." I am not even playing with you guys, I legit felt instantly good about my project. Then it dawned on me what he had said, I dashed to my computer and added this paragraph. Proof, you guys, it really works, it worked on me.

This page has been left blank for your planning or notes

THE MEXICAN MARTINI
Cocktail | Shake | Martini Glass | 1 serving
Welcome to being the parent of a teen. Prepare yourself for large amounts of eye rolling, emotional outbursts, thoughts of running away... and that is just the parents!

INGREDIENTS
2 oz. Tequila
1 oz. Orange liqueur
1 oz. Orange juice
0.5 oz. Lime juice + wedge
0.5 oz. Olive brine
Ice
Black lava salt
3 Blue cheese stuffed olives

STEP 1
Run the wedge of a lime around the rim of your glass then dip in crushed black lava salt. Place in the freezer to frost.

STEP 2
Add your ingredients to your shaker with ice and shake for a count of 10, vigorously.

STEP 3
Strain into your frosted glass and garnish with stuffed blue cheese olives on a toothpick. Enjoy!

I always use a cognac infused orange liqueur and a tequila blanca

This is neither a Mexican drink nor a martini. This is totally an Austin libation. There are a few restaurants in town who claim to make the best one... after drinking at multiple establishments, having others make their interpretations for me, I played around and determined this recipe to be the best ratios and ingredients. What do you think?

(This page has been left
blank for your planning
or notes)

CUCUMBER COLLINS
Cocktail | Shake | Collins Glass | 1 serving
You'll know when you have become a real parent when you have flipped off your kids (at least once) behind their backs.

INGREDIENTS
4 - quarter inch-thick slices of Cucumber + 2 to 6 extra slices for garnish
2 tsp. Sugar
0.5 of a Lemon juiced
2 oz. Hendricks Gin
Sparkling water
Ice

STEP 1
Slice the cucumber into four-quarter inch-thick slices and then slice each wheel again into fourths.

STEP 2
Place cucumber pieces into bottom of shaker with two teaspoons of sugar and muddle *(see pg. 30 for directions)* with the wooden handle of a spoon.

STEP 3
Add juice from 0.5 of a lemon, ice and 2 ounces of gin to the muddling and shake to a count of 10.

STEP 5
Strain into frosted glass full of ice, top off with sparkling water. Garnish with two slices of cucumber. Enjoy!

VARIATION:
Need a little heat? Try adding fresh sliced jalapenos in step three and again in step five's garnish with extra thin slices.

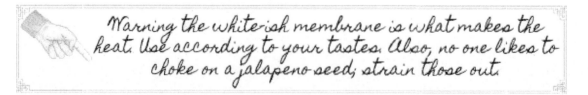

Warning the white-ish membrane is what makes the heat. Use according to your tastes. Also, no one likes to choke on a jalapeno seed; strain those out.

CARRYTAIL VARIATION:
Choosing either the regular or spicy Collins to make, omit the gin and use more sparkling water instead.

This page has been left blank for your planning or notes

PRIMAVERA
Carrytail| Shake | Coupe Glass | 1 serving

Loving your child is natural. But parenting without letting your occasional hate show is a true work of art.

INGREDIENTS
7-8 Blueberries + 3 extra for garnish
Rosemary sprig leaves + extra top sprig
1 oz. Lemon juice
1 tsp. Agave nectar
Sparkling water
Ice
Fine strainer

STEP 1
Muddle *(see pg. 30 for directions)* 7-8 blueberries and leaves of rosemary sprig with lemon juice at the bottom of your shaker with the handle of a wooden spoon.

STEP 2
Add your agave nectar and ice then shake for a count of 10.

STEP 3
Fine strain into your glass layering with sparkling water.

STEP 4
String two blueberries onto your toothpick, then the rosemary sprig, and finally your third blueberry to sandwich the sprig in-between the berries. Garnish your drink and enjoy.

COCKTAIL VARIATIONS:
Add 1 to 2 ounces of gin depending on how crazy you want to go. I'd recommend the Austin gin. Also, try skipping the sparkling water and use sparkling wine. I love Cava from Spain!

HOW OTHER PARENTS DO IT

Experts Be Damned

"I do not care what the experts say, I lavish my kid with as much praise as I can. You want to know why? Because this world is a tough and scary enough place with people just waiting to tear you down. My kid is going to know beyond a shadow of a doubt that I am always rooting for them. My parents gave me up and no one ever wanted me. No one cheered me on. I never want that for my kid. They need to know that at least one person in this world thinks that they are good, kind and smart. It just feels right to tell them that."

-Kathy - mom of one teen, Denver, Co.

CHAPTER 9: FRIGHTFUL FIFTEENS AND THE SCANDALOUS SIXTEENS

"Listen, honey, nobody knows how to raise a teenager…you just live through it, and one day they are people." -Momonymous

When you have unpleasantly shocking fifteen-year-olds running around with sixteen-year-olds showing questionable morals, you'll be glad you read this chapter on:

- Nothing new here
- Secret lives
- Showing up
- 11 Authentic listening steps for diffusion
- 3 Types of teen discipline

Don't forget to pre-game with the On Trend (with variations), Touchwood, or a Siciliano.

WELCOME TO THE JUNGLE

This is the reincarnation of the two-year-old-stage, except now your teens are blessed with narcissism that could annihilate the cosmos.

Often when raising a teenager, you can feel like you are alone in the chaos that your child is creating. I can assure you that is absolutely not the case. There is nothing new in the world of parenting a teen. 2,400 years ago, Aristotle wrote that teenagers are "fickle in their desires" as ephemeral as they are fiery. He lived 62 years during 384-322 BC. At the time he wrote that he was a 41-year-old tutoring an annoying thirteen-year-old who would be known later as Alexander the Great.

453 years ago, Shakespeare wrote that teen brains were (loosely quoted) "boiled and therefore adolescence was only good for getting preggers, embarrassing the family, stealing and fighting." This sounds exactly like what my husband said last week.

Sometimes you look at them and they come off as articulate grown-ups that you think have all the pieces - but then sometimes, without warning, they obviously don't. Unbelievably annoying and scary things happen… it can drive you to want to live under the bedcovers and drink from the bottle.

These are the years their brains are under major construction and the best thing you can do besides vacations, as it is not always the best idea to leave teens alone, is to give yourself liquid courage. Because they will drain every last bit out of you. Who needs Halloween? Every day with a teen is like that, they are either tricking or treating you.

Odd as it may seem, especially after an introduction like the one above, I prefer my teens to their formerly cute munchkin self.

There are numerous days where my feelings about them are mercurial – ever changing. But overall, the older they get the more I enjoy them. The conversations, when they happen, get deeper. Watching them form their own opinions in adulthood, is also breathtakingly beautiful. It is like meeting a tiger in the jungle – a majestic beast that is a true wonder, terrifying you with each move. And yet, though you are pissing your pants frozen with fear, you love getting that memorable up-close-personal look at a natural wonder.

I read this incredible book by Barbara Strauch, titled The Primal Teen. In layman's terms, she wrote about the research on teen brains. These researchers found that unique human functions like reasoning, motivation, and judgment and how they involve our seriously large prefrontal cortex which is developed oh so G.R.A.D.U.A.L.L.Y during adolescence. Even though your teen can think on a higher level, they also have a difficult time making decisions on rationality.

Imagine the impact of drugs and alcohol on this slowly growing, constantly changing brain! [Don't do it. Stay away from it until you are an adult.]

The thing about teens is that whilst their pre-frontal cortex isn't as well developed biologically as they'd like to think, they know it all! They are living a secret life, in which none of us know anything about. Truly terrifying. I have met a lot of parents who will argue this with me because they have got the perfect kid. Well either their world doesn't match up with their perceived reality, or the teen is going to wait to rebel until they are out of the house as an adult. It happens to all of us at some point in our lives. We question the reality that we have been brought up with and need to test new a hypothesis of how life could be. It is a good thing, though they go through it in a horrible way, making it very difficult to parent.

WHY LIVE A SECRET LIFE?

In chapter two, I told you that kids lie to avoid punishment and/or disappointing parents. Why we lie as we grow still holds true with these two reasons but after seven years of age, there are one or two additional reasons.

1. They become so adroit at that manipulation; their brain is used to telling falsehoods. They really don't know how to turn it off without some new cognitive behavioral training (i.e., more reward for being truthful than lying).

2. Information aversion. Do you ever start to ignore messages, news, social media because you're tired of the negative information coming in? This holds true for teens too. There is psychological pain with admitting to the things you're doing that won't be approved. It is easier to avoid the truth than to own up to things you might be doing that aren't good decisions.

The problem with this secret life is that horrible experiences will happen that we, as the parents, know nothing about it. This secretive world fills them up with mines waiting to be triggered that unknowing well-meaning parents' step on and are suddenly blown up. There is no stopping the secret life. Sometimes it'll feel like it is best if secret lives stayed secret. Allowing me and other parents to live in Ostrich Effect, where you stick your head in the sand to avoid reality. If this were the healthy choice this book would have just one chapter.

OWNING YOUR OWN

The way through it is to realize you yourself can transform your own triggers by owning them. Find the meaning in the pain you are experiencing, blaming not the past or present but finding a way to grow from the life experience. Then take it a step further and have an open dialogue with your teens. The first 100 times will be difficult and embarrassing to talk openly about all your self-work.

Eventually, the law of reciprocity will come into play.

When you authentically relate to your kiddos about struggling to transform yourself, they see two things from you:
1. Family is there for it all. To listen, love and support. Family = safe place.
2. There is no isolation in the struggle.
Talking things out helps teens to learn to slow down their emotional reactions and process, and set-

up healthy personal boundaries. Talking is problem-solving and sharing burdens makes them lighter.

A WORD OF WARNING.

You have to be really real in your forgiveness of self and others. Remember, it isn't a lesson you are teaching, no lectures, sermons, or pontifications. Focus on you and your own growth, otherwise, it will backfire.

Don't you love books that tell you how to theoretically identify and deal with something? It seems to be rare that you get a map of how you deal with the situation while it is happening.

There are typically two different types of reactions to anger, explosion or implosion. When you are in the middle of a heated discussion with your teen, one person might be exploding while the other is imploding and if other children or adults are in the room, they too are having their own reactions that will come out in aftershock ripples.

Ooohhhh, dear parent… I know this is the hardest testament to you but whatever you do, try not to do it in anger. This advice is coming to you from a mom who spent the first twelve years of parenting in an anger strong enough to create its own black hole for the universe to get sucked through.

I'm a slow learner, apparently, but I have learned two vital lessons that resolve most parenting crises.
- "A soft answer turns away wrath."
- "Don't answer a fool according to his folly."

This is often hard to do in the moment and I don't always muster self-control, so I implement environmental control. If a child has volcanically erupted and pushed me to my breaking point when I want to raise my voice, throw something, or slam a door …*it is amazing how quickly these learning humans can put you into a Jack Nicolson from The Shining-worthy moment…*, I grit my teeth and say, "I need a minute!" while stiffly walking to a closet. There, I do whatever I can to calm myself. Deep breathing …*thank G-d for yoga and Lamaze classes…*, prayer, meditation, cry, call my husband, or shoot a quick text to a fellow mom (that also has teenagers of the same gender that I can be brutally honest with about my child).

I have two such girlfriends, they have been a true lifeline during some of the most harrowing moments when my husband would be out of town or in a meeting. I highly recommend that you get at least one friend who has a child the same age and same gender. This is not to be biased; you should have lots of friends that have kids in all stages of development and opposite genders from yours but have at least one friend who is in the same boat as you that you can be honest with about the good, the bad, and the ugly.

In the heat of these Vesuvius-like moments, there are two components I have had to drill into my head to remember.

1. The teens are doing their job, exploring boundaries.
2. Your job is to figure out their "why" and then help them navigate it.

SO, WHAT IS THE HEART ISSUE HERE?

Sometimes you can recognize their manipulation before you talk to them and address it, but sometimes they are triggered by something you don't quite know. Perhaps, from that secret life, we talked about?

In chapter three, we talked about authentic listening and the steps to follow - here I want to mention the diffusion steps for authentic listening during conflict. These steps are not just useful for raising kids but also during those "wonderful" moments when you have to approach another parent about your kid, their kid, or one of the other million excruciating reasons you will have to have a difficult conversation with another parent, or when you have to watch another parent parent your kid. In conjunction with using a sh*t sandwich, positive - negative - positive, these steps may help to diffuse the situation and feel more non-combative.

11 Authentic Listening Steps for Diffusion Tactics:

1. Look the person in the eyes (if culturally and/or spectrum appropriate).
2. Let them say their piece.
3. Repeat what you heard verbatim, if possible.
4. They concur what you have repeated or correct what was misunderstood.
5. Repeat back the misunderstanding, correcting if needed.
6. Speak about what it means to you.
7. They repeat back what your spoken feelings are.
8. Confirm or correct what they repeated.
9. What should/can we do about the situation (e.g., what you need from me and what I can offer)?
10. Repeat what each other said about what they can do better from step 9.
11. Thank them for listening and talking about what is on your/their heart. Offer forgiveness IF you are ready.

A couple more details that I would add for achieving optimum conflict resolution is:
1. Don't Interrupt
Establish the rule that you don't interrupt when someone is speaking. Even if you feel like what they are saying is false. There will be an opportunity to address it later.

When we started implementing these resolution tactics, I used to be "hands off" when it was between the kids or their friends. My thinking was that they needed to learn from experience not from me facilitating everything. After a couple of times, I noticed that when my kids interrupt each other while they are trying to tell their side of events the one interrupted felt devalued and the situation never really came to a closure. Now with this rule in place, and me there to enforce it things began to resolve more quickly. When everyone gets to fully say their side, they feel heard. Most of the time that is all anyone wants.

2.   Hold Space

This is a three-step process. First, we have to make room for what was learned by each party during the listening process, then own our part in the hurt, and finally create a plan for dealing with it afterward.

This part is a life-long practice in progress, you never really perfect it. It is a new way to communicate. Expect that it is going to be difficult and give yourself and others grace for working through it. Each time you try you will get better at it and your relationships will blossom. It is difficult to listen to someone tell their side of something while you sit there feeling unable to defend yourself. In the beginning, there is a lot of just waiting for your turn to speak, but eventually with enough time of sitting and waiting for the heated reactions cool down and everyone will start learning to listen and be slow to speak. – Hallelujah!

What does creating a plan from step nine involve?

Apologizing. If you plan on just saying "I'm sorry", it won't work. It feels insincere with a lack of accountability. Try instead: "I understand that XYZ hurt you. I did not want XYZ to happen/I could have done/said that better. Will you forgive me?"

No one is required to say "yes", just don't say "no", it is either a "yes", or "I am going to need some time to think about this".

As the adult, a key thing to model for them is when you are not ready in that moment to offer forgiveness, don't forget to go back when you are ready and offer the forgiveness openly. Also, don't forget to go back and follow up by making amends when you are to blame by however much. Try not to let it fester or be ignored. This is a valuable lesson for your kids to deal with the uncomfortable as soon as they can and not let guilt or shame set into an unbreakable silence that kills you. Have the tough talks and have them quickly.

One of the most common mistakes we all contribute to in the breakdown of relationships is to assume that the other party just knows. My mother …*who would die if she knew I told you she said a *lean in close and whisper* swear word *gasp! feigning shock and dismay*…* always taught me how to spell assume by using the old colloquialism of "to assume just makes an ass out of you and me".

98% [Yes, I just inserted a completely over the top made up statistic to prove a point] of relationship breakdown is made by a lack of communicating authentically. This includes listening and not assuming. Start over-communicating your thoughts and needs non-violently, truly listening to what another person is telling you and I fu**ing promise you that you will be more successful in relationships.

DISCIPLINING THREE TYPES OF TEENS

It is difficult to write anything specific to help clarify because each situation and child will be wholly different. However, I think the best guideline is to remember that everything you are doing is for the greater good of teaching your child who will be a future adult.

Think through the filter of how this will help them in the future. Sometimes we are too quick to react, especially in anger. The older they get the more it becomes even more clear that we were never in control. That is a terrifying reality.

I have one teen who between the ages of 12 to 17 became apathetic to anything being taken away for punishment. Hardest five years of my life trying to figure out how to motivate and discipline. I have one child who will do everything to not lose anything. They are a hell of an easier kid to motivate and discipline. We have had kids pass through our care who would rather climb a tree and lie to avoid trouble than stand on the ground and tell the truth. Facing the consequences was a fate worse than death. These kids were just as hard but on an entirely different level as my first.

WHAT TO DO?

I want to emphasize that for those that are looking for a one size fits all punishment it doesn't work that way. Every person is different not only in personality but in the seasons of their life. What works once may not work again. What works for one probably won't work for the other. Below, I am going to list the three types of kids that I have experience with. I trust that you will be able to keep trying if it doesn't seem to be working for you. Know that my prayers are with you – because I know firsthand how hard this sh*t is.

With child A, my apathetic one, I had to find out their "why" of what they did, then decide what I wanted them to learn from this experience. What were the natural consequences of that situation? More times than not that is more than enough. If something more was needed, then I thought about what would fit the crime. For example, dumping over port-o-potties = volunteer to clean up public toilets. Stealing = return property and money to co., time spent without item that matches stolen item, volunteer at a shelter of those less fortunate. Bullying = serving the person bullied or serving a group of people less fortunate.

Child B is not really much of a problem. Usually, stern looks - even his sister wakes him into making more conscious choices. *We will see how long that lasts.*

Child C, the ones who would prefer to lie, I had to make it okay for them to tell the truth. I had to practice this stepford-ish face, devoid of emotion and judgment, to coax the truth of them. I would set up scenarios for my kids to tell me shocking truths in front of them, so they would see that I meant what I said about being able to tell me anything.

I know, I can hear some of you saying, "But how does that teach them anything, Nicole?!"
Do you recall chapter 2 on lying? There is a serious heart issue here. This child is going to need guidance back to understanding that they have had either too sharp of a stick or too much of a carrot for lying. It is going to be a long and difficult road back to figuring out how to breakdown their barriers. Then, it will be an equally long road of why they do what they do and how to build back up the character that you desire in your child.

In those moments, I had to choose relationships overall. I had to make a safe place for them to tell me all of their junk. After that was established, then I could set up a more Child A-like discipline scenario.

If you find yourself here as a parent, my heart goes out to you. When we, as parents, are faced with apathy and lying it is easy to start beating yourself up for not knowing what to do or handling something wrong. Remember you are enough for your child and always have been. Have courage, and when you know better do better.

This page has been left blank for your planning or notes)

ON TREND

Carrytail | Shake | Tumbler Glass | 1 serving

My kid is turning out to be just like me. Well played karma. Well played.

INGREDIENTS
3 Sliced fresh strawberries
1 oz. Cranberry juice
0.5 of a Lemon juiced
3 Fresh raspberries
1 tsp. Honey
Ginger ale
Ice
Fine strainer

STEP 1
With the handle of a wooden spoon, muddle *(see pg. 30 for directions)* strawberries with cranberry and lemon juice in your shaker.

STEP 2
Add raspberries and ice to shake for a count of 10. Fine strain into a frosted glass.

STEP 3
Top off with ginger ale. Garnish with a strawberry and drizzled honey to enjoy.

The "On Trend" name comes from the freedom to substitute whatever fresh berries are in season.

This page has been left blank for your planning or notes

TOUCHWOOD
Cocktail | Stir | Coupe Glass | 1 serving
I can't wait for the day when I can drink with my kids. Not because of them.

INGREDIENTS
Splash of dry vermouth [just enough to rinse around and coat the inside of your glass]
1 ½ oz. Single malt whisk(e)y
1/3 oz. Amaro
1/3 oz Sherry
1 turn Cracked black pepper
Lemon wheel slice for garnish
Ice

STEP 1
Frost your whisk(e)y glass.

STEP 2
Stir all ingredients, except the vermouth, into another glass with ice.

STEP 3
Rinse your frosted glass with vermouth. Just enough to coat inner glass sides and bottom

STEP 4
Strain your chilled ingredients into your vermouth rinsed frosted glass.

STEP 5
Garnish with lemon wheel slice and enjoy.

Mathew Follent created this recipe and won the 2016 "Perfect Blend Competition" using Auchentoshan Three Wood Lowland whisky.

This page has been left blank for your planning or notes

SICILIANO
Cocktail | Shake | Brandy Glass | 1 serving
Half of the day I wonder if it is too late for coffee and the other half I wonder if it is too early for alcohol.

INGREDIENTS
2 oz. Sweet red vermouth
1.5 oz. Amaro
1.5 oz. Strong brewed coffee cooled
1 oz. Agave nectar
Club soda or sparkling water
Orange wheel for garnish
Ice

STEP 1
Mix all ingredients except club soda and orange wheel in your shaker.

STEP 2
Add ice to your shaker and shake vigorously for a count of 10.

STEP 3
Garnish with an orange wheel inside your glass and then strain into your frosted glass, top with club soda to enjoy.

HOW OTHER PARENTS DO IT:

Parenting Goal: Don't Raise Little Pricks

"When my children go to friends' houses, I am told they are always bonnie. But the faery folk must get ahold of them by the time they get home because they aren't. They are little asses.

By my third teen, I have realized that there is a competition to see who can drive me crazy first. I must work to not take it personally. Hard to do when you have a little prick throwing their stuff down or slamming doors when they come home from work or school.

Because I love them, I'll ask, "Hey, are you ok. Want to talk?" "NO. I DON'T WANT TO TALK TO YOU MOM." See, you hear about the scary stuff that goes on in the world with kids, cutting or drugs, suicide and I just want them to know that I am here. The bloody situation escalates.

The trick is to keep my answers – responses short. Short responses and walking away keeps everyone alive. The majority of the time, they come down and apologize. It's a process and we are all trying to just survive here.

Also, my recommendation is to get a dog when you have a teen. It is important to have at least one person happy to see you each day."
-Esme - mum of three teens, transplanted in Houston, TX

(This page has been left blank for your planning or notes)

CHAPTER 10: THE SOMETIMES-SALACIOUS SEVENTEENS AND EDIFIED EIGHTEENS

"What's parenting like? It is like trying to stand up in a hammock without spilling your wine."-Momonymous

If you are in shock at overhearing how vulgar your seventeen-year-old talks to their friends, many of them turn an uplifting corner by the time they turn eighteen – hang tight. In the meantime, let's equip ourselves with:

- How your parenting increases lying
- Dangers of comparisons
- Positivity – a new moral correctness

But first maybe we should make an Uzum Fizz (with variation), Fraise Martini (with more glorious variation), or a stout Smog Cutter might do the trick.

These capricious years seem to change weekly. When they first enter the teen years, it feels like they are changing their attitude minute by minute. But, by the time they turn eighteen, it slows down a little and becomes more of a week by a few weeks of choices being changed. It is slightly similar to being drunk on a merry-go-round. Slow, fast, dizzying, and with annoying music.

To be raw and truthful with you guys, this has been the hardest years to let them flounder. Especially when I look at my youngest knowing I will have to go through it all over again. I remind myself every morning that these are the baby-adult steps. The thing that makes this the hardest now is that the stakes are higher, and the delusion of control is absent. The good news seems to be that they are slightly less rebellious at the age of eighteen than they were at eleven.

TEAR DOWN THE STONEWALL

Remember when we talked about how all teens have a secret life in chapter nine? Wouldn't you like to know what part of your parenting is the cause?

First, I have to say that finding out the cause does not keep you from having a kid who lies – it just means you have a higher probability that they will lie to you less and stop lying earlier. It should also be said that no one should ever state that ALL kids are ALWAYS a CERTAIN way. As much as we are alike, we still have anomalies of nature.

What are you doing to create more lies and deception? Inflexibility. There are usually three categories of parenting that you can place almost anyone into.

The first, are the parents who in good nature set up a lot of rules. Sometimes these parents put up all the NO NO's to stay away from. In hopes of helping clearly guide the children into understanding the expectations. Some take it further and put a positive spin on their rules, same gig, just said in a different way. For example, instead of saying "don't lie", they use "We Do Forgiveness". Either way, the rules are phrased to the key component in what there is a copious amount of. I'll call this group the "Rulers".

The second, are the parents who in their best efforts to craft a friendship bond with their kid they don't have any rules. They might have come from incredibly stern parents themselves and they seek to correct what was done to them by taking a divergent route. This group will be known as the "Friends".

The problem with the Rulers is that when you have more than three to five rules, it is incredibly difficult to enforce them all. Because the rules are not being enforced, it leaves room for deception. Kids end up learning early on two things, (1) You are not going to be able to keep track of every rule they are breaking and (2) What you don't find out, can't disappoint you.

With the Friends group, when there are no boundaries while growing up, how can a child learn to test them? How are they supposed to discover what the boundaries are for themselves? It might seem like a more harmonious household to live in mutual regard. "You stay out of my personal space and I will stay out of yours", but all that your kid will feel for the majority of the time is that you don't care. If you don't care, why should they? Hardly seems fair, does it...? Most likely, you probably care quite a bit.

Both sets of parents create teens who feel it is necessary to lie about almost everything. Not out of disrespect, but for an easier time for both you and them. Who wants to waste energy on a parent who is not going to budge anyway? The same way with the "Friend Parent", who doesn't seem to care enough to set down any guidelines? The scary thing about these kids is that they will lie about things that don't need to lie about. It is as if they have been deceiving so long, they can't remember what it feels like to tell the truth.

The third category of parents are the ones who get lied to significantly less. Rebellion will still happen, but it also burns out quicker, and the kids from these parents come clean more quickly and easily. These parents seem to have two things in common. First, they set only a few expectations down and because there are less than five rules, they can easily enforce them. However, the aspect to these parents is that they are open to listening. There are discussions, sometimes heated but ultimately, they will hear their kid's point of view without stonewalling them.

The second is that their "rules" don't focus on the desired behavior. The thought process is that rules-based behavior creates an atmosphere for herding sheep. "Be Respectful" requires zero creative and original thinking. In turn, this can develop a distaste in the rule follower you are raising. Why should they follow your rules, enticing rebellion? If you are currently on broken-record-repeat of any rule you have... take a moment to find the reason behind the rule. Has it ever been explained?

This third group of parents focuses instead on value-based behavior. They convey their values behind the rules. This allows for the child to think for themselves helping them to see the reason in following someone else's contrived rule.

For example, the rule "Have Respect" would have the value explained in situations as they arise (not all at once):

We value respect in this family, so we don't:
- Interrupt each other when talking
- Get up from the table until everyone is finished

But we do:
- Return items immediately after we borrow them
- Leave a space nicer than we found it

Their whole time as a child is learning how to conceptualize deep, complex and arbitrary concepts like respect from you. First, they learn what the word is, then they learn what it looks like to have it and give it, by the time they are an adult, hopefully, they are able to build on those initial blocks and understand its deeper meaning. However, none of that will happen quickly or without much ado.

It'd be nice if lying didn't need to be a part of the equation, but I will take being able to work together as a consolation prize if it means that my children learn it.

THE SLOW DEATH OF COMPARISONS

Parenting, like gardening, means that you are doing the best you can. It doesn't mean that the outcome will always be Instagram photo ready.

Most of us are probably nodding our head in agreement, but it can be difficult to live this truth in the day to day gatherings with other parents. We tend to internalize that we may not be doing it right, and when we show up to the public, we always want to put our best foot forward, best photos, best bragging right stories, etc.

I am not trying to morally correct you for "thinking positive – showing positive". I do think that parenting can be the toughest mirror to investigate. We can create little depressing islands of loneliness comparing our family to another family. It'd be great if we could all remind ourselves that we don't have the full story when looking through the open curtains of the window that the happy family has provided for us.

When we grant another human the right to their life and their choices, they can be disappointing because it is not what we would choose. But if you can be brave enough to be open with another parent about the mistakes you have learned from, it will be your scars, your jagged edges, that create texture for another person to grab onto and connect to what makes your story yours. By the same token, you can connect with them in their trials.

Don't get me twisted though, I am not suggesting that we all swing the pendulum the other way and only show the dirt under the rug; however, life is too short to always toe the party-face line.

THE FATE OF BAD EMOTIONS

I love how Susan David; a Harvard psychologist states in her TED talk that we often have "dead people's goals". In life we often just want those "bad" feelings to go away, but only dead people don't have feelings or stress. We have boxed ourselves into using "Be Positive" as a new form of moral correctness. We are often judging ourselves and others for having the "bad – sad – mad – grief" emotions. I get it. When another friend is relating something uncomfortably negative about their situation, I often want to hug it away and rush to a bumper sticker solution, pointing out where it "really will work out – it is going to be okay – you can do this!" It is easier to push aside tough emotions than to sit there and be okay with stress and discomfort.

These "bad" emotions are normal and are inherently valuable. These are the ones that give us the capacity to develop skills to deal with the real world as it is, not as we wish it to be.

Tough emotions are our ticket to living life.

When I started figuring these pieces out, I found that all I really need to do was sit with it, there is no need to fix it. If I am having an emotion the opposite of happiness, it is ok. I can stop, look around inside of myself and see what it is that I am reacting to. Once recognized, I can either do something about it, or not, depending on what seems right at that time.

Basically, I have learned that it is okay to not know what to do or have the right thing to say to myself or a friend who is suffering. The most powerful gift I can give to myself or a friend is to simply sit holding zero expectations.

TO BE OR NOT TO BE

This entire book has been about how-to parent to all the different age-stages that occur, however, you will notice that in these last few chapters more and more it is about leading by example. The process of parenting is to always be leading by example; some years are heavier handed than others. As your children age, you never stop parenting. It just becomes more obvious that all you can do is show the way through your own actions.

Another parent-friend is not going to make the same choices as you and that can give one pause, "how much do I really want to be exposed to these choices/lifestyles/opinions". However, it could be an opportunity to show your kids how to approach all things in love. Even to those other parents whom you love to hate.

Leading by example you can demonstrate how to sit in silence, not cutting disagreeable people off in their diatribe speeches ...*unless they are toxic... close the door on that -ish already...* but allowing them to feel welcome in all of their crazy – for who are we if we only love those whom we already love?

Rest assured that if "Freakonomics" has taught us anything it is that our kids will learn even from bad parents. Most of your parenting job will be done by how you show up in life and if that is the case it might be time to worry more about your own self and how you are leading by example.

This page has been left blank for your planning or notes

UZUM FIZZ
Carrytail | Blend & Shake | Highball Glass | 1 serving
Don't yell at your kids ever. Instead, lean in close and whisper. It's much scarier.

INGREDIENTS
2.5 oz. Red grape puree
4 oz. Cucumber water
0.25 oz. Lemon juice
0.5 oz. Thyme syrup *(see pg. 20 for directions)*
Ice

STEP 1
Steep 2 cups of water with one small cucumber that has been sliced into ¼ inch disks for at least 30 minutes. Then take a large handful of red seedless grapes and puree them in a blender.

STEP 2
All ingredients go into the shaker and dry shake (this means without ice).

STEP 3
Fill your glass with ice and alternate layers with juice and sparkling water. Enjoy!

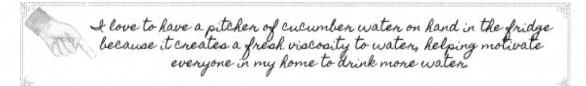

I love to have a pitcher of cucumber water on hand in the fridge because it creates a fresh viscosity to water, helping motivate everyone in my home to drink more water.

COCTAIL VARIATION:
1 -2 oz vodka as an add-in

This page has been left blank for your planning or notes

FRAISE MARTINI
Cocktail | Shake | Martini Glass | 1 serving
You're making it difficult for me to be the parent I always imagined I'd be.

INGREDIENTS
1.5 oz. Vodka
2 oz. Pineapple juice
4 Strawberries
1 oz. Crème de Fraise
Top sprig of basil
Ice

STEP 1
Muddle *(see pg. 30 for directions)* 3 strawberries with pineapple juice at the bottom of your shaker.

STEP 2
Add your vodka and crème de fraise and dry shake (this is without ice).

STEP 3
Add ice to your shakers concoction and shake vigorously for a count of 10.

STEP 4
Fine strain into your frosted glass.

STEP 5
Garnish with a strawberry and slapped tip sprig of basil. Enjoy.

COCKTAIL VARIATION:
THE FRENCH MARTINI
Keep all proportions the same. Switch out your strawberries for raspberries. And instead of Crème de Fraise (a strawberry liquor) use a Chambord (a raspberry liquor). Omit the basil and you have an entirely different taste to enjoy.

This page has been left blank for your planning or notes

SMOG CUTTER
Cocktail | Shake | Beer Goblet | 1 serving

For when it is time to cut through the bullsh*t; realize that loving your child means you don't worry about their opinion of you.

INGREDIENTS
1.5 oz. Tequila
6 Thin slices of ginger
1 1/3 oz. Simple syrup *(see pg. 30 for directions)*
2/3 oz. Lemon juice
Dark Mexican lager beer
Ice

STEP 1
Muddle *(see pg. 30 for directions)* the ginger at the bottom of your shaker.

STEP 2
Add syrup, lemon juice, tequila to the shaker with ice and shake vigorously for a count of 10.

STEP 3
Strain into your frosted glass, topping off with the dark Mexican lager beer to enjoy.

 My favorite dark Mexican Lager is Modelo Negra.

HOW OTHER PARENTS DO IT:

The Most Important Book You Should Read

"Some parents mistakenly think that Dr. Seuss is only to be read to little children, but now, as they become baby adults it is the perfect time to revisit. Especially, Oh, The Places You'll Go!

'You'll be on your way up you'll be seeing great sights! You'll join the highfliers who soar to high heights. Except when you don't because sometimes you won't.'

It is too easy to know how and what to do with your vast years of experience. Learn to listen. Accept what your little adult wants to do even if it is the opposite of what they said when they were little and daydreaming. Even if it is not what you want to tell your friends when they ask what your high school graduate is doing now with their life.

How to support a budding adult. Realizing that their choices are their path. This is where you need to be okay with being confident that it will all be okay. It is important to teach this all the way along but especially reinforce at this point of parenting that life is not measured in success or failures. Enjoy the success when they come and let them drive you to learn when the failures come. Not if they come, but when they come. Because they do for everyone."

-Ed - dad of two adults, grandpa of 1 baby, Houston, TX

CHAPTER 11: NEOPHYTE NINETEENS AND THE TOLERANT TWENTIES

"Between the adolescence and baby adulthood is a place of rapid changes. For example, a parent will age 20 years. "-Dadonymous

While your nineteen-year-old starts to develop new beliefs and skills and your twenty-year-old sows promise of allowing other opinions to exist we are going to talk about:

- The brand-new adult
- Grace, not perfection
- Acceptance
- Gravity problems
- The benefits of finding problems, not solutions

I can't wait for you to discover the delicious libations in this chapter! We have the Brandy Crusta, Cuban Reverie, and the Golden Buddha (with divine variations)

NEWLY ADULTING

When your adult child says they love you and make time for you it feels better than winning the lottery. Watching your new adult struggle to make life-choices feels like the seventh level of hell. *"do you know what I'd do if I was your age and had these opportunities splayed out before me like a banquet?!"*

This age-stage, more than others, parents feel like time and advantages are being wasted on the young. To go to college or not. To work or not. To travel or not. To take a gap year or not. The choices are innumerous.

All we see is that all of it is right in front of them for the taking. If they'd let you, you'd supply them with a map of the perfectly illuminated path that you have already forged. Yet, you are almost completely out of control. You don't get to decide; you barely get an opinion. Mostly you watch, smile and wait. Hopefully, you have set up enough trust between the two of you to establish authentic honesty. You'll offer support where you can but not too much because you are still trying to push them out of the nest to get them to try to fly, right?

I have heard they eventually figure it all out; but damn! If it isn't like trying to watch your toddler stumble to walk.

A lot of us fall into the death spirals of comparison. ...*Diamond's daughter is getting into MIT while your little Ben has decided he is not going to go to school and he is not sure what he is going to do other than work at his current job at the marina's gas station...* It can feel like a personal parenting failure and embarrassment.

As painful as it is to watch your child struggle, this is what parent-love is all about. Letting them have the freedom to make their own choices because they do learn best through the mistakes you don't want to let them make. Take heart and gird yourself with the findings from the 1945 study the "Candle Problem", it shows that you can't generate creative cognitive problem solving if you have never had the opportunity. No amount of reward incentives will increase it, it comes from an environment of pure self-direction.

I've learned to sit on my hands or leave the room when the new adults start spouting "ideas" of how it is going to work out. I find I naturally place fault within myself for my shortcomings as a parent and think of ways to help course correct their future. However, no one told me that this clobber continued well past eighteen. I guess I conned myself into thinking that legal adulthood was when the mantel lifted.

This has been a season of learning to slowly unclench my fist. The one that is holding on to the former beliefs of how it should look and be at this stage. Let go. Outstretch your arms, lower your shoulders, lift your face ...*feels like we are in a yoga class!..*, open your hands and let go as they toddle into adulthood.

PUBLIC CORRECTION

Not the time or the place. This is your adult child if they slip up and say something not so kosher at a party, take a breath and remember they are an adult and at a party with you. Your hostility is due to your embarrassment from what others think, which is not really your kid's problem.

I love when my precocious almost twenty-year-old gives me ample opportunities to breathe deep and keep my mouth shut when she says or does something at a party that I find not the most pleasing. It is a strenuous exercise because I want to immediately correct. I have to remember she is not my little monkey; the time is forgone for me to constantly correct; she will have to feel the shame from others and not just from me jumping into over-parent. This is their adult life now not mine to control and steer. My practice has become to realize that not everything needs to be solved right away.

STANDARD OF GRACE NOT PERFECTION

I love taking drives in our part of Austin, Texas. It is the beginning of the hill country and the views are picturesque. One of my favorite podcasts to listen to while driving is "Hidden Brain" with Shankar Vedantam. I find so many parallels to raising a family in it. A common theme I see with the kiddos who pass through our door is the struggle with perfection, and in several podcasts, it has been addressed. Apparently, this issue isn't just common amongst kids but people in general.

Somewhere throughout our society, we have been teaching that there is only one way to do life; or there is only one perfect you. There is one way to get to what your passion is meant to be. This is a complete fallacy.

Think about what we are saying to our children. The line of ludicrous bull that we have been fed. Essentially, they need to choose the one map to navigate their entire life when they do not have all the information on how it is going to turn out.

Remember the comedian, Bill Engvall, who always ended his jokes with "Here's your sign"? The term for creating a strategic design system for finding your way around an area, a city, building, or subway is called "wayfinding". I know, makes total sense, right? Here's your sign for finding your way around.

Where is this in life?

This term, wayfinding is not just a tool for figuring out where to go. It can also be a metaphor for getting comfortable with the fact you may not just have one destination in life.

There is more than one right answer to what your life looks like. It starts by stopping to ask the wrong questions, "how do I figure that one best optimal version of me?", "how could I be sure?" These kinds of questions don't allow for room for error; we may try things that eventually don't work out.

The only way to parent at this point is to have discussions about the changes you are making in your life. The lessons you are learning. Baby-adults more often than not have stopped listening to their parents because most parents have stopped growing. You cannot pour new wine into an old wine skin. New adulthood is the new wine and your life and sage advice is the old wine skin. This world – their world, is fast-paced and changing. Our advice might not always apply. By the way, it has always been this way since the dawn of time. "The old way" is not a new saying.

WHAT DO YOU NEED TO DO?

Life equals constant change. How different would things be if instead of making your ENTIRE career path at eighteen, we instead teach our kids to partake in the odyssey of life – who is Odysseus without his journey? A fun thought experiment you can try is practicing with yourself to come up with three variations of yourself. Learn to take one step at a time. Figure out a little something about the direction you are trying; seeing how a few things happen, again and again until you arrive at an iteration that brings you joy. Following that path until change is needed again because if you are not changing, you are stagnating. Remember the last time you walked past a stinky pond without flowing water... yeah, that's stagnate. What a wonderful leading example that your adult children can observe and learn to follow.

This acceptance can create happiness. In contrast to the loaded questions of "Is this really your passion?" "Is this it what you want to do with your life...forever?" The thief of your peace and happiness is the unknown factors that create the future possible you.

Regret is absolute poison. It is how we become complacent in life. Learning to flame the desire to "do" and "experiment" instead of "wish" is the only way that I know how to lead my kids by example. Showing them how to push past fears and insecurities by sometimes "flying by the seat of my pants".

GRAVITY PROBLEMS

What are gravity problems? It is something that you cannot do anything about. These problems when unrecognized are the bane of our anxiety until we learn to determine that it is a circumstance, not a problem.

Learn to teach your adult kids to understand and see if the problems they think they have are not actionable. Can't make money as a painter? This is a gravity problem. When faced with this kind of dilemma, we must learn either how to make money for rent and carve out time for painting as a hobby. When we learn to categorize overwhelming problems as gravity, we free our thought processes to circumnavigate to a compromised solution.

My kids have just read this section and started singing this song we sang to them in preschool. It is silly. But wow, there really is truth to it.

In the song "We're Going on a Bear Hunt", we come across crazy natural obstacles that "we can't go over it, we can't go under it, we can't go around it, we've got to GO THROUGH IT!" Gravity problems are much the same way, something you have to work through, not wish it away.

PROBLEM FINDING

Rudderlessness comes from pressure to find the right decision and ideal life. You feel you are not where you want to be which creates a cycle of beating yourself up for not knowing where you want to go or what your true purpose is.

Tech engineers have an excellent term for it, "design thinking". Before you can problem solve, try problem finding. What is the right problem to be working on?

There is a course at Stanford called "Designing Our Life". It focuses on discovering that life has either one of two problems, tame and wild.
1. Tame problems are ones we know how to solve with a simple straightforward solution.
2. Wild problem is where the criteria are changing all the time. The status is never stable. Like marriage, and kid raising, etc.

The course then teaches approaching life by implementing the empirical process. Pursuing multiple ideas with trial prototypes and testing something out to see the possible success rate. Can you imagine the relief this creates for people? The ability to say, there are many things I am interested in not just one passion that will be my life's career. New career fields spring up overnight. If people are scared to learn new things, they won't be able to take advantage of the future. How can we begin to relate this to our children? We need to be the brave pioneers leading the way.

We live in a time when the days of working for one company, having one vocation path are dying out. My father's advice is ringing in my ears, though I do not think this was the application he meant it for, "be so organized, you are flexible". We need to cultivate more adaptability. Both in our education and preparation for ourselves, as well as our kids. How would things change for our future if young adults have the opportunity to seek out and learn transferable skills rather than one vocation with advancement? It changes the perspective we parents have from fear for our newly graduated children to liberating hope.

This page has been left blank for your planning or notes

BRANDY CRUSTA
Cocktail | Stir | Old Fashioned – Rocks Glass | 1 serving

Humans have ten million brain cells. Each child takes three million cells and tweens take seventeen million. Leaving us in the negative, that explains everything.

INGREDIENTS
2 oz. Cognac
1 -2 Dashes Curacao (or .25 tsp. orange liquor)
0.5 tsp. Simple syrup *(see pg. 30 for directions)*
0.25 tsp. Lemon juice + cut a wide peel to line inside of glass
1 – 2 Dashes Angostura bitters (depending on taste, some recommend 1 dash Angostura and 1 dash bittercube bolivar but this can be difficult to find)
Enough sugar to coat the outside of glass
Ice

STEP 1
Rub a lemon wedge around the outside of your wine glass or whiskey glass about an inch wide from lip down. Dip into the fine sugar to coat the outside. Place in your freezer to frost while you finish making the rest of the cocktail.

STEP 2
Stir the rest of the ingredients in another glass with ice until well chilled.

STEP 3
Peel a wide swath of a lemon and line the inside of your frosted-sugared glass.

STEP 4
Pour your chilled ingredients into your lined-frosted-sugared glass, enjoying every bit of your awesomely ostentatious drink.

Be extra careful as to not get any sugar on the tippy top of the rim or inside the glass as this will destroy the careful balance of flavors you are building.

Placing the sugar-coated glass in the freezer is the secret success to getting your sugar to really crust onto your glass, and it is the first hallmark that makes this drink so special. Bartenders would judge other bartenders for their ability to skillfully coat the outside of a glass.

This wide lemon peel lining the inside of your glass is the second hallmark of a true Brandy Crusta. If you order this drink from a bar and they don't do this...then you can secretly judge that bar's lack of care for a true Brandy Crusta.

This page has been left blank for your planning or notes

CUBAN REVERIE
Cocktail | Shake | Poco Grande Glass | 1 serving

Parenting is emotional. It is bottling up and shaking it like a good cocktail. Sweet but it will knock you on your a**.

INGREDIENTS
1.5 oz. Dark Rum
1 oz. Lime juice
1 oz. Simple syrup *(see pg. 30 for directions)*
8 Mint leaves + extra
1 Dash Angostura bitters
Sparkling wine
Ice
Fine strainer

STEP1
With a wooden spoon handle, muddle *(see pg. 30 for directions)* together the lime juice, simple syrup, and mint leaves at the bottom of your cocktail shaker.

STEP 2
Pour in the rum, bitters, and ice. Shake for a count of 10.

STEP 3
Fine strain into your frosted glass, alternating with sparkling wine.

STEP 4
Garnish with the leaves off the tip of mint sprig and slap them to release their oils, enjoy!

This page has been left blank for your planning or notes

GOLDEN BUDDHA

Carrytail | Shake | Coupe Glass | 1 serving

That awkward moment when you're not sure if you actually have free time or you're just forgetting everything.

INGREDIENTS

1 tsp. Chopped lemongrass
0.5 oz. Vanilla syrup *(see pg. 20 for directions)*
0.5 oz. Lemon juice
4 oz. Steeped and cooled jasmine tea
2 oz. Lychee juice
1 Lychee to muddle
Ice
Fine strainer

STEP 1

Muddle *(see pg. 30 for directions)* lychee, lemongrass, and lemon juice at the bottom of your shaker with a wooden spoon handle.

STEP 2

Add your lychee juice, jasmine tea, vanilla syrup, and ice. Shake for a count of 10.

STEP 3

Fine strain into your frosted glass and enjoy.

VARIATIONS:

Add any cold brew tea of your choice.

For a warmer version keep tea warm and dry shake ingredients together, following the same steps just omitting the ice.

For a less Carrytail version, add 1 – 2 ounces of whisky.

 Lychees can be found fresh in the produce of an Asian market or canned in your grocer's international aisle

HOW OTHER PARENTS DO IT:

Ignorance Is Bliss

"Some of the hardest years are between eighteen and twenty-one. You think that a burden has been lifted when they turn eighteen, but surprise, it is not. It only gets scarier until they are totally legal at twenty-one. And I think the only way through it is to realize you just don't need to know. Ignorance is bliss, and when you know too much, prayer and cocktails are the best comfort."
– Rebecca - 3 kids 22, 27, & 30, Tulsa, OK.

This page has been left blank for your planning or notes)

CHAPTER 12: TERRIFYING TWENTY-ONES

"I want to thank you, parents, for your patience, your encouragement, your strength, your generosity, your unswerving love, and for those six little words that helped me through so many trying times... 'Because. I. said. So. That's why!'" -Sophie adult daughter to my friend Jude from NJ

Right before your twenty-one-year-old strikes terror into your heart make sure you read this chapter on the last four lessons to convey:

- Faithfulness in the small things
- Thoughts are power
- Habit growth
- Put it down

Before or after reading, don't forget to imbibe with the Distrito Federal (and its variation the Manhattan), Fig Manhattan (my all-time personal favorite in good times and bad!), and the Parkside (with her variation).

ADULTING: THE LAST FOUR LESSONS

The irony of turning twenty-one is that it is equally terrifying for both you the parent and the kid adult. Your heavy lifting as a parent is done and now your relationship trumps all. I realize now how my oldest is almost ready to be a fully-fledged adult, and I am fooling myself with how ready I think I am for her to be one. One night I woke up in legit sweats thinking about these four lessons that I really am just figuring out for myself. I fretfully wonder if I have learned them enough to be implementing them in my own life conveying them in time to my little girl. Time will tell.

#1 FAITHFUL IN THE SMALL THINGS

No one wakes up one day with the intention of blowing up their life. What happens is that we make tiny decisions every hour of the day that have the potential to destroy or build our lives. It is in these tiny decisions that we make have small changes that can develop small habits leading to our ability to take action or not.

How easily our thoughts can defeat us.

We checkout when it is overwhelming. And our brains protect us from doing things that release the hormones associated with fear and distress.

We are all one thought away from being a success or failure in every aspect of our lives. One thought can change the choice of action you will make in your relationships or your work. That action can determine the level of fear or bravery you enter your next steps, setting the patterns and habits from which you will take the rest of your steps.

I have found that in everything in life if I can show up and be faithful in the small things this clears the way for me to almost always knock out the big things. When I need to square off to a big scary job, I take it one section at a time. When self-defeating thoughts float into my consciousness, I repeat (often out loud!) "That is a future problem that will be solved by future Nicole." Yes, I am fully aware of how crazy that sounds, but it helps me focus on what I can manage. With building successes of managing those small sections the closer the completion of the "big scary job" comes into view.

Faithfulness in the small things is not just about creating bite-size chunks for large problems. It is also about your daily habits.

It might seem like a large leap from making your bed to feeling confident to tackle a daunting project, but it isn't. The small everyday habits you show fidelity to help clear the white noise in your head. If your visual space has some semblance to order you feel free to do the work that requires deep thinking. It uniquely helps lessen the blow of failures. If you come home from an unsuccessful sucky day to a clean kitchen and made bed, you feel a new seed of empowerment start to grow. This gives you the strength to take on the next day knowing that you didn't fail at everything, you have at least one win for the day.

#2 THOUGHT IS POWER

Daniel Kahneman is famous for writing about our two systems of thought in his book, <u>Thinking Fast Thinking Slow</u>. We all have and use both fast thinking, the automatic way we intuit the world around us, and our slow thinking, the deliberate effort and time we take to think critically.

When I grasped that I had two systems of thought, at first, I concerned myself with trying to improve one thought system over the other. It probably took me longer than most to figure out that my focus should have been on recognizing when I was using a certain system.

We need both systems of thought to engage in life. The relationship between the two is what influences how we behave. Our fast thinking system is effortless freeing up our day, whereas our slow thinking system is for our deep thinking - our important work.

The problem lies with when we use our fast thinking-impulsive-system for the majority of our decision making.

Making choices and informed decisions takes a lot of prefrontal cortex work, it can be draining. Often times we think in our easiest system, fast thinking. We jump to conclusions without looking for bias or correlations.

There are two thought patterns in our fast thinking where all of us could use a little more awareness.

The first is referred to as our "Cognitive Illusion Traps." These are what we think we know based on what we experience. However, we are not taking the time to listen and think critically. For example, when your mom (your grammy, your auntie, your uncle, and all your friends) told you, "I warned you about that bad boyfriend, but you dated him anyway." You dated him because your personal experience with that person told you the opposite of the advice given by everyone else. You assumed it was them that just didn't know him like you did. If slow thinking were used here, you'd spend time considering other outside opinions and try to view that "boy" more objectively.

The second fast thinking danger zone area is the "Sunk Cost Fallacy". This is when you stick with a bad choice you have made because you have already sunk so much time, effort, and money into a situation. Like when you are at a concert and even though it is not the best music of all time most of us will choose to continue to sit through it because we drove all the way there and spent the massive dough to see it. When I looked at where I was doing this in my life, it started to become easier to recognize it as using the wrong thought system. All it would take for me was to get up and change my situation; consequently, adding happier future memories for truly little extra money or time.

#3 HABIT GROWTH

We tell ourselves that mistakes are the worst thing we can make happen in life. This internal mantra ends up driving the creativity out of people. Creativity is doing despite fear. Adults spend a lot of time waiting to be inspired, whereas young children just do.

We can find ourselves trapped in a "Knowledge Action Gap". Where we know what we need to do to change our circumstances, but we just can't seem to get ourselves to do it.

A few times in our married life, my husband and I have had financial stresses. No big surprises there, most of us do as adults. One time, in particular, bills would come in and it was far easier to pick it up from the mailbox and deposit the envelopes with pertinent warnings into another box inside the house to ignore. We were in survival mode and those envelopes threatened our very existence.

The true way out of more stress was to sit down together, open them up, and set up plans to tackle the incoming problems. We chose to mimic cartoon ostriches, sticking our heads in the sand and ignoring the difficulties facing us. There was nothing anyone could tell us differently, but mostly because they didn't know what was going on and the deeper into insurmountable stress, we drove ourselves.

Until one day, well past our breaking point, we sat down batched our woes into piles and took baby steps to tackling each one. It was painful. It took forever. In the end, the action felt better than inaction.

Mel Robbins, the on-air CNN commentator, went through some harrowing moments in her life and thereafter sank into a bitter depression. From this, she discovered that self-motivation was never around when she needed it. Each night she wound up promising herself that tomorrow was going to be the day she started her "new and improved self". But it never happened.

A pattern of five seconds was the amount of time she needed between her ideas spawning and hopping into action. If given any more time, she would bail on the idea altogether. She began breaking her first bad habit of hitting the snooze button to go back to her dreary "weep and sleep" by counting backwards from five to one and jump out of bed like a rocket.

"How can it be that childishly simple?" She went on a quest to find the science behind it. Now, she speaks around the world spreading her Start Ritual, 5…4…3…2…1!

Our habits, feelings, and emotions are in the basal ganglia, in the deep center of our brain – the cerebral cortex. These feelings will continue to occur in enclosed loops until they are broken.

When we count backwards, we disrupt those habit loops and move our brain. This activates the prefrontal cortex which is where our thoughts happen. Counting backwards lands on the number one, priming us for a single moment of courage.

If we count upwards, we won't feel the same spurt of energy because we can keep counting. Numbers are infinite. It doesn't require thought to count upwards but going backwards does. It prompts us to a move to action and heightened focus.

One small window of five seconds or less can move you to create action. Don't give yourself time to hang out in the feelings of being overwhelmed and afraid to start or change. This gives self-doubt a foothold to creep in and paralyze you.

Count backwards and move. Change your life.

We, as adults, get stuck in habits thinking we need to reach deep within ourselves to find the motivation that we need to rebuild ourselves into a new and better version of ourselves. When no, that is not true.

Firstly, we must accept who we are as a person. When we are ready to move beyond that and change ourselves, we need only to act not just wait for motivation to show up.

However, getting to that action can feel like a non-starter. Having our head-in-the-sand sounds like the best course of action to take. Priming our minds to jump the habit loop is where we can kick start ourselves with counting down and doing the action. Don't allow time, self-doubt, or all the reasons why you can't get it done. Whatever it is, losing weight, paying overdue bills, writing a book, …*these all sound vaguely specific to me…anyone else?!...* these goals require more action than thought.

Yes, it will eventually become a habit. But that is what you want, to develop better habits. At this moment you need to interrupt your autopilot signals. And the way to do that is as simple as pretending you are five-year-old pretending that you are a rocket ship ready to blast off.

#4 PUT IT DOWN

Anyone living in the world after 1984 has been experiencing an increase in two developments, the satisfaction of instant gratification, and wanting to make a difference.

If you want it, click it and you have it. We all have these super cool small shiny smart devices that fit in the palm of our hands, controlling our entire world engagement.

In these modern times, your life seems to not be meaningful if you are not out there "making a difference" in the world.

Simon Sinek gave an interview on Inside IQ Quest with Tom Bilyeu about how now, more than ever, we struggle with the lack of deep meaningful connections and relationships as adults. We have this growing lack of developing our skill sets in dealing with difficult and uncomfortable situations.

Our coping mechanism has become turning to a device that gives us an easy hit of dopamine.

We are on them all the time. That constant engagement has decreased the satisfaction we feel in life and relationships. We spend vast amounts of detrimental time looking through the open window of other people's lives and compare ourselves and our choices to it. We see people doing amazing things and having the time of their lives. This constant engagement ultimately takes up all of our thought space, killing time for innovation and building trust with others that are physically in our lives.

There is a small change you can give yourself and it will rock your world. Put it down.

What does it really mean to make a difference in the world? I think a lot of people want to be a part of something bigger than themselves and they want to do it in a BIG way. I think that the smallest offering is being overlooked; how we engage with others around us.

If we were to put down our devices and look up, we'd see the biggest impact that we could make. Having time to hold a small space for innocuous connections with those around us. Try smiling at a stranger. This small practice demonstrates compassion.

What would change in our world if we experienced the ripple effect of compassion?

What about when no one is around? Are you allowed to be on your device? Sure, but still make time to have it set down more than in your hand. This space you give yourself is perfect for you to give yourself the gift of time to think by yourself. Having time to sit and think is when we experience innovation. Think of it as a spa minute for your brain.

This page has been left blank for your planning or notes

DISTRITO FEDERAL
Cocktail | Shake | Coupe Glass | 1 serving
After all this parenting, I think I am better suited to be a hostage negotiator.

INGREDIENTS
2 oz. Tequila blanca
1 oz. Sweet vermouth
2 Dashes orange bitters
Lime wheel slice &/or cherry for garnish
Ice

STEP 1
Stir all ingredients in your shaker with ice.

STEP 2
Pour into your frosted glass. Garnish with a lime wheel &/or dark cherry.

COCKTAIL VARIATION:
THE MANHATTAN
2 oz. Whisk(e)y or bourbon
1 Dash Angostura bitters
¾ oz. Sweet red vermouth
Follow the same steps as the D.F. cocktail above.

This page has been left blank for your planning or notes

FIG MANHATTAN
Cocktail | Shake | Coupe Glass | 1 serving
My kids are the reason I wake up each morning, the reason I breathe …. and why my hair is falling out, my house is a mess, and I am crazy.

INGREDIENTS
0.75 oz. Sweet Vermouth
2.5 oz. Bourbon
1.5 oz. Thyme simple syrup *(see pg. 30 for directions)*
1 – 2 Dashes orange bitters
1 Egg white
2 tsp. Fig preserves + ¼ tsp. for meringue
¼ tsp. Cream of tartar
Ice
Fine strainer

Directions for Meringue:

STEP 1
Whisk together one egg white, 1 tsp. of fig preserve and cream of tartar until soft – bartenders peaks form.

STEP 2
Set aside until cocktail is poured.

Directions for Cocktail:

STEP 1
Pour vermouth, bourbon, thyme syrup, bitters into your shaker, and 2 tsp of fig preserves.

STEP 2
Shake ingredients with ice vigorously for a count of 10.

STEP 3
Fine strain into a chilled glass

STEP 4
Top with the previously made meringue and enjoy!

Cream of Tartar is to help stiffen the egg white. Bartenders peaks are much softer than the whipped meringue that you create for a dessert. This is because you want to be able to drink the meringue not eat it.

This page has been left
blank for your planning
or notes

PARKSIDE
Carrytail | Shake | Martini Glass | 1 serving
Once upon a time, I was the perfect parent, but then I had children.

INGREDIENTS
4 oz. Cranberry juice
0.5 Lime juiced
2 Basil leaves
Ice
Agave
Crushed Salt for rim
Sparkling water
4 – 6 Frozen whole cranberries for garnish

STEP 1
Rim a glass with agave nectar and salt. Place in the freezer to frost the glass and harden the nectar.

STEP 2
Muddle *(see pg. 30 for directions)* basil leaves with lime juice in a shaker.

STEP 3
Pour in cranberry juice and shake with ice for a count of 10. Pour into the frosted and rimmed glass. Top off with sparkling water and garnish with frozen cranberries. Enjoy!

VARIATION:
Add in 1 to 2 oz. tequila

HOW OTHER PARENTS DO IT:

At Some Point, You Miss The Mess.

"In two weeks, my kid will turn 21. I do not know how we have gotten here. It literally has been the scariest roller coaster ride from 'Oh, yeah my kid is doing great; studying to be a ...' to trying to decide if boarding school is a better option.

I feel like that guy at the end of YouTube who's fainted a couple of times in the middle of a roller coaster, woke up to yell that he wanted a breakup to his significant other and now at the end of the ride, while it is pulling up to release the lap bar, sits there with dried tears streaked across his face. Thankful that the ride is over... that is how this is feeling for me. I have learned to be REALLY THANKFUL for the small things, like still no cavities, no babies, and only needing to pick him up once from the police station. I have learned, the less I know, the less I yell, and I feel like that is the healthiest decision I have made for him and me.

I have accepted that he doesn't want me around for a lot of his decision making. Lately, the times we are together are mostly sweet. I really find I want to do his laundry and clean his apartment...I miss the gnarly orange chip stains on the sofa. When the f*&k did that happen?"
Jennifer - mom of one baby-adult, Austin, TX

CHAPTER 13: PARADOXICAL TIMES AFTER 21
"The first 40 years of parenting are always the hardest." -Dadonymous

These are the years when you have those self-contradictory talks with your adult kid. When you tell them all the things you couldn't because you didn't want them to do it. In this chapter, we are going to focus on:

- The art of conversing
- Asking meaningful questions

We are going to do it a little different in this chapter, with each of my favorite Prohibition's cocktail recipes and histories, I am going to give you four invasive questions to ask your kiddo and divulge your inner true self with them. The excellent giggle juice libations are, Between the sheets, 12-mile limit, Southside, Sidecar (and a variation), Glazed Maple Old Fashioned (with even more controversial variations)

Welcome to life with a child older than twenty-one. Some of you will be empty nesting, while others still raising the rest of the brood. During these moments with your new adult friend, you will start to hear more and more of all that was previously forbidden. You are going to need a stiff drink. Especially when they move back home. The best part between their 20's to their 60's is you might get the chance to watch them grow into their own parenthood. Just like your parents did. You'll find yourself wondering if they are great because of what you did or was it what you didn't do?

What is the best way to connect with any human being? Have a conversation.

This seems like, and is, a simple thing to do, but we seem incapable of really listening or asking questions that engage. A high school teacher, Paul Barnwall, wrote a piece for the Atlantic positing that Conversational Competence, the ability to have interpersonal communication, is the single most overlooked skill not being taught today. He became aware of how destitute our youth are after he assigned his students a communications project and they performed badly.

Barnwall's students were supposed to conduct interviews with fellow students following up on some of the major social injustice issues facing our society today. Apparently, the students struggled to engage in active face to face conversation.

Social media and technology have given us wonderful platforms to raise awareness of social injustice issues from around the world. Most people can enjoy a lively debate and carry on a conversation through using a few characters. The question needs to be asked; is it robbing us of the ability to balance between talking and listening?

When did it become difficult to have conversations with another person despite having differing opinions? How often do you feel you have had one of those great talks where you feel engaged in a sustained conversation, understanding another person deeply and felt your point of view was truly heard?

The Pew research center is churning out studies that show a correlation between the amount of daily texts/tweets/posts a person sends vs. the actual face to face time conversations. You and Barnwall already know its results are sadly lacking.

Celeste Headlee, a long-time radio host, brought up some interesting points during her TedXCreative talk. She called bullsh*t on all the time that is spent trying to teach people how to "look" like we are paying attention as an important skill when conversating. "If you are really paying attention, why do you need to know how to show you are paying attention?" That can't be what is missing from the art of good conversation.

There two parts to conversation - listening and talking. I think the talking part with your kids can be really engaging if you learn to ask compelling questions.

Steven Covey wrote in his book, <u>The 7 Habits of Highly Effective People</u>, about people needing to listen with the intent to understand not with the intent to reply. I think if we can master just that one concept we will be doing alright.

THE ART OF CONVERSATIONS

The way in which we ask questions in a conversation illicit more engagement and helps us in understanding our kiddos better. The two most common mistakes people make are not asking enough open-ended questions and not waiting for the other person to answer.

When you ask leading questions, often it is perceived by the answer-ee as though they are not really needed in this conversation. It seems that the talking is more for the other person to hear their own voice.

WHAT ARE LEADING QUESTIONS

These questions don't require much thought to respond past a "yes" or a "no". If I ask you "Have you ever been on a rollercoaster of love?" you'd probably respond with "Yes, I have", or "No, I haven't". That is an example of how dead-end a leading question can be.

I am not saying to never use them in conversation – that'd be absurd. Leading questions can be a charming way into starting a conversation.

The complication that gums us up from keeping the flow going is when we don't follow up. If we ask our initial question of, "Have you ever been on a rollercoaster of love?" and then after the person's short response you then also follow it up with, "How did that go?", or "How'd that make you feel?" this is what will create a small opportunity for growth in the conversation.

HOW LONG DO I WAIT?

Often, we don't wait for responses long enough. Conversation is not an easy thing to do, it requires focus and energy. Questions that ask us to divulge deeper answers take thought and we need some time to come up with an answer.

Give a person at least one minute of thought time. Yes, this will feel uncomfortable but if you can become comfortable with the awkward silence it will be worth it.

Recall the adage, "still waters run deep".

In our fast-paced world, it is difficult to allow silence to linger while waiting. We think, "maybe they need help… I will clarify it." They don't. If they did, they would ask. They need time to gauge their answer, they might feel strange at someone genuinely wanting to hear what they have to say. Though your instincts are crying out to goad them along, refuse to follow them. This goading only serves to shut people down instead.

Wait. Wait. Wait in the stillness of the air hanging between you two.

If it is longer than two-minutes you might want to check their pulse, or perhaps offer up something personal on your end as a white flag signaling, "hey, here is my vulnerability and you are safe to be vulnerable with me".

The counterpart of conversation, responding, has a profound mistake that almost all of us make.

The part that makes conversation so hard is that it requires focus, and our brains like to wander. Inevitably when someone is talking it will spark a memory of how you went through the very same thing but acquired a greater understanding or underwent more suffering. It could remind you of a very important question or point to make that as a parent it is your duty to relay to your child.

Don't mention it, at least not yet.

What we can do is remember the words of ancient teachings like Buddha, "If your mouth is open, you are not learning", or from the 18th chapter of the book of Proverbs, "If one gives an answer before he hears, it is his folly and shame". Come to think of it, perhaps this learning to listen thing is just a human condition problem, not a recent one spurred by technology.

It is vital to remember with your kids (and all people in your life) to stay present to what they are saying. When those memories or points come floating into your head, let them flow right back out. You need to be presently listening to what is being said to you in order to engage and not give a lecture or show off how cool you used to be.

You cannot multitask and converse.

One technique that I learned from a new friend I met, while traveling with my son in Mexico, was to close my eyes and take a deep breath before responding. It felt weird, and it looks weird watching it, but damn if it didn't work to calm the mind and remain present.

Getting excited and waiting for your turn to talk is such an easy place to get tripped up because it is every human being's desire to be heard and be known. If you are not getting enough of this in your life, you easily commit this conversation killer. If you have found yourself guilty of tripping up here just take it as proof that you, like everyone else, need to find fulfillment in this area.

A technique that I learned from a software engineer was when you are trying to tackle a vexing problem, do the opposite of what you are wanting. The way I apply it here is if I am talking until, I am blue in the face, I take that very moment to realize I need to be heard. Instead of forging ahead, trying to be heard, I do the opposite and offer the opportunity to the other people in the room, sitting back and listening to them.

Be prepared to be astounded when you start practicing this kindness, everyone is walking around with something secretly amazing about them.

WHAT ARE SOME RIVETING QUESTIONS WE SHOULD ASK?

I have written a list of four excellent base questions that you can modify or build on when paired with a prohibition cocktail. These need not be asked verbatim. There are no rules that they have to go as paired. Ask 'em how you want, when you want.

I find they can be deeply personal and probing.

A little liquid courage to loosen up the tongue is a great accompaniment and you also may not always want the answers you get from your kids. Heck, you learned that a long time ago, right?!

WHY PROHIBITION DRINKS?

In the late 19th century, the "drys" – those against the selling and consuming of alcohol, were led by very pietistic protestants, who led a tirade on curing the ill society struggling with divorce and violence. They succeeded in getting laws passed to have a nationwide constitutional ban on the production, importation, transportation, and the sale of alcoholic beverages from 1920 to 1933.

They mainly inadvertently succeeded in giving rise to rebellion and sales on the black market. I saved these cocktails until now just for this section thinking it was a cheeky way to celebrate getting to know your kid better. Instead of quoting Mom and Dad anonymous, I put in little snippets of the stories behind the naming of each prohibition drinks.

This page has been left
blank for your planning
or notes)

BETWEEN THE SHEETS
Cocktail | Shake | Coupe Glass | 1 serving
The origin story of this cocktail is that in the early '20s this aperitif was the preferred consumption of French painted ladies. Ooh la la!

INGREDIENTS
0.75 oz. Rum
0.75 oz. Cognac
0.75 oz. Orange liqueur
1 tsp. Lemon juice
Orange peel + lighter
Ice

STEP 1
Shake all ingredients with ice vigorously for a count of 10.

STEP 2
Strain into your frosted glass

STEP 3
Peel a wide swath of orange peel and squeeze oils then using a lighter or a match to ignite the oils on the peel to warm up and open the flavors, drop the peel into your libation before enjoying.

I WANT TO KNOW YOU QUESTIONS:
- What is a relationship deal breaker for you?
- How many times have you been in love, what have those times taught you?
- What makes someone instantly more attractive?
- What is the stupidest thing you have done for love?

This page has been left blank for your planning or notes

12-MILE LIMIT
Cocktail | Shake | Highball Glass | 1 serving

During the era, U.S. law stated that the consumption of alcohol was banned up to a dozen miles beyond its shores. This is where boat bars got their infamous start. No wonder that this extreme measure created a mass rebellion… and a prosperous black market.

INGREDIENTS
1 oz. Rum
1/2 oz. Whisk(e)y or bourbon
1/2 oz Cognac
1/2 oz. Grenadine
1/2 oz. Lemon juice + peel
Ice

STEP 1
Add all ingredients in your shaker with ice and shake vigorously for a count of 10.

STEP 2
Strain into your frosted glass and garnish with a lemon peel. Enjoy!

I WANT TO KNOW YOU QUESTIONS:
- What should I know about you that I'd never ask?
- What was the last mistake you made that you are sure you will make again?
- What is one fear you know is holding you back?
- What is the most illegal thing you have done?

The Scots (Canadians & Japanese) spell it whisky and the Irish (& Americans) spell it whiskey. This difference in the spelling comes from the translations of the word from the Scottish and Irish Gaelic. The Gaelic origin word means, "Water of Life."

This page has been left
blank for your planning
or notes

THE SOUTHSIDE
Cocktail | Shake | Martini Glass | 1 serving

Historical rumor has it that this was the favored drink of the infamous crime czar, Al Capone, whose gang dominated Chicago's southside. Maybe it was because he needed something that could be made and be imbibed quickly in case he needed a fast getaway.

INGREDIENTS
2 oz. Gin
0.75 oz. Lime juice + peel
1 oz. Simple syrup *(see pg. 30 for directions)*
3 to 4 oz. Soda water
2 mint leaves for garnish
Ice

STEP 1
Add gin, lime juice, and simple syrup to your shaker.

STEP 2
Shake vigorously with ice for a count of 10.

STEP 3
Strain into your frosted glass and garnish with 2 slapped mint leaves, and 2 lime wheels before enjoying.

I WANT TO KNOW YOU QUESTIONS:
- Tell me two truths and one lie.
- What is a misconception about you that others often have?
- When did you screw everything up, but no one ever found out that it was you?
- What irrational fear do you have/had?

(This page has been left blank for your planning or notes)

SIDE CAR
Cocktail | Shake | Coupe Glass | 1 serving

History is always disputed I think because it is passed down as stories. My favorite is that this drink's roots are from the Big Easy, New Orleans, a large and once pirating seaport in the south of the U.S. This drink reminds me of what should represent America, a melting pot of ingenuity and capitalism. Bartenders would combine a heavy pour of French cognac and a little dash of Spanish curacao with a smidge of citrus helping to keep those sailors from succumbing to scurvy and keep returning to their port for some "healing".

INGREDIENTS
2 oz. Cognac
0.75 oz. Lime juice + wheel
0.75 oz. Orange liquor
Ice
Sugar for garnish

STEP 1
Shake liquids in your shaker with ice for a count of 10.

STEP 2
Strain into a frosted glass with 1/4 rimmed in sugar. Garnish with a thin lime wheel slice or an orange peel twist to enjoy.

VARIATION:
The Original Sidecar uses the ingredients brandy, curacao and lemon juice, following the same instructions. Just changing these two citrus juices can give the drink distinctly different flavors.

I WANT TO KNOW YOU QUESTIONS:
- Who is your most interesting friend?
- What is the best/worst advice you have received?
- In a group of friends', what role do you play?
- Who and what is the most ridiculous thing someone has tricked you into believing?

(This page has been left blank for your planning or notes)

GLAZED MAPLE OLD FASHIONED
Cocktail | Build | Old Fashioned – Rocks Glass | 1 serving

Pre-dating the motor car and President Lincoln, this drink has withstood the test of time. Created in an old gentlemen's club where men rarely behaved like the namesake. Surviving the changing of the guard this drink has become a favorite among us ladies too (whether we behave like it or not).

INGREDIENTS
2 tsp. Maple syrup
1 tsp. Water
1 Dash Angostura bitters
2 oz. Bourbon
1 Orange peel slice
1 Brandied cherry
1 large craft ice sphere

STEP 1
Mix maple syrup, water, and bitters in your glass until well-blended.

STEP 2
Place a large ice sphere in your glass add the orange peel and pour your bourbon on top.

STEP 3
Add your brandied cherry and swirl your glass around to combine the flavors you have built just before sipping to enjoy.

If I never see ANOTHER fake brightly colored maraschino cherry again, it will be too soon. If the bar you are at serves you this style of cherry with your O.F. send it back and leave. Immediately. Splurge on yourself and get the REAL super good kind from a liquor store. I usually buy the Luxardo brand.

Water in your bourbon? What are you crazy?! Adding a SMIDGEN of water to your bourbon/whiskey is the same chemistry as adding oxygen to your red wine. It opens the flavors. The reason to use those big obnoxious craft ice shapes is so that the ice is slow melting and doesn't water that deliciousness down.

If you do not have mold to make these giant ice shapes, skip adding the water and use a couple regular ice cubes.

COCKTAIL VARIATIONS:
THE O.G.
Instead of maple syrup use traditional syrup or make a brown sugar syrup.

HOTLY DEBATED VERSION:
Use 0.5 oz. maraschino liqueur instead of any simple syrup. Use two dashes orange bitters and one dash Angostura bitter.

BREAKING ALL THE RULES VERSION:
Follow any recipe but omit angostura and orange bitters and instead use 1 to 2 dashes of Peychaud's bitters (this gives it a floral flavor).

I WANT TO KNOW YOU QUESTIONS:
- What is the most valuable lesson you have learned from a mistake?
- What piece of advice, had you followed it, would have you in an entirely different place today?
- If you could know the absolute total truth to one question what would you ask?
- If you could change one thing in your history what would it be?

HOW OTHER PARENTS DO IT:

Just Embrace It.

"This is definitely the hardest year. My daughter just turned 31 and she is grown and knows it all and true my daughter is wise beyond her years, but I am her mother no matter how old she gets. She still unknowingly tries to manipulate me like she did when she was two. It is weird to be still setting boundaries for her at this age, but I must.

You just never ever stop parenting. Your parenting just has to become super covert. Just like when they were little they get hurt, and desperately need you. You think you are at the point where you can be friends and talk about things in your life and, true, to some extent you can. But, if it is going to be a topic that directly touches their childhood, like discussing your spouse or your sex life, forget it. They are not going to be understanding at all.

When your children are adults, you can have a deeper relationship with them, but you can't have the same level of adult intimacy that you can with other adults who were never under your authority. I never understood why parents will say their kid is their best friend. Why put that kind of pressure on your kid regardless of their age? If they are an eight-year-old, isn't it weird to be friends with someone who is not as mentally developed as you are? When you are both full grown adults, there is an element to your relationship that will stay parental; why wish that away?

My advice? Get your own friends (of all ages) to busy yourself with. Always make time for your kid when they need you. Let your kid see you out and living! They still need an example from you that life doesn't end at 50, it is just beginning!"
-June - Mom of a 31-year old, Boston, MA.

This page has been left blank for your planning or notes

CHAPTER 14: JUBILANT CELEBRATIONS

"It is like no one in my family appreciates that I stayed up all night overthinking things for them." -
Momonymous

This is the perfect chapter to talk about:

- Why we celebrate
- Importance of friends
- Party formulas perfect for hosting

I have put my 16 best punch and bubbly recipes (both cocktail & carrytails) in this section divided by the season they correspond well with.

SUMMER
Punchy Pineapple, Punch & Judy, Soixante Quinze, Garden Sangria
AUTUMN
Orange-Apple Cider, Barry Hall Punch, Kentucky Fizz, Autumn Berry Bouch
WINTER
Winter Plum Punch, Feurzangen Bowle, Smoothbore 125, Cranbucha
SPRING
Spring Brunch Punch, Frontier Punch, French 77, Bouchy

ABOVE GROUND

About the only conversation my husband and I had on expectations we had before we started our family journey was sitting on a couch one evening at his grandparents' house, just after one of their large parties. We were watching them chat with the last few remaining guests who were not overnighting. He leaned over to me and whispered, "This is what I want for now until we grow old and crunchy. I want our lives and home full of family, friends, and community."

I could not have agreed more.

Everywhere we have moved, in every size house or income, or lack of house and income, we have always had open doors, welcomed family and friends, and found a way to build a community around us. We still pale in comparison to his 86-year-old grandmother's social calendar, but we are forever striving to make each person who walks through our doors wanted and valued and then party until everything breaks.

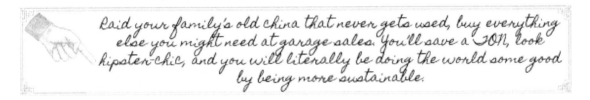

Raid your family's old china that never gets used, buy everything else you might need at garage sales. You'll save a TON, look hipster-chic, and you will literally be doing the world some good by being more sustainable.

Our motto for hosting gatherings has always been: "Each day above ground is a good day to celebrate."

We don't worry about which friend-set is going to clash with which. We don't worry about how well we know someone before inviting them over. It is always an unspoken rule that our guests are always welcome to invite a couple of their friends. However, the most important expectation that we set for ourselves is that we don't stress over how clean our house is… just kidding I totally stress over it every time. When we committed to welcoming all through our doors, we committed.

LACK OF COMMUNITIES

Loneliness is a real problem across the globe. It is not for a lack of being able to be instantly connected to old friends or like-minded groups. There is a deepening chasm between each of us. The pressure to "sell to the public" that your life is worthy, is too great. We end up missing the connections with another person because we are too busy making sure no one sees the sadness we may feel.

Suicide rates are among the highest in our youths right now.

I am not going to pretend to even know the true root cause or the right solution. I can only comment on what I see in my world of raising kids, living life, and having teens and young adults walk through our door to sit a spell – I feel it is a failure to connect. To deeply and authentically connect to someone.

We can go through our entire day having lots of happy conversations with everyone we meet. We can smile at the stranger walking down the sidewalk, but when was the last time you shared your heart with your friends in person? When was the last time you listened to your friends' heart? How about beyond your friends?

I think that there are a lot of us who are out there connecting. However, there are seven billion plus people on the planet and the suicide rates are still rising. For me, this means there is room for growth in this area.

I wanted to start with my children. I wanted to show them what it means to be active in our community. Not with busyness… we are all busy, with genuine love and connection. I probably fall short every day. I might even have a friend reading this hurt that I haven't contacted them in a while – know that I am trying every day to be better.

There are three women who have been influential in teaching me about the importance of friends and community.

I have the fondest memories from when I was young of my mother playing on a volleyball league, throwing parties with friends and laughing big. I wanted to be her. She was beautiful and knew how to have fun.

My grandmother-in-law has always taught me that as a woman who moves around a lot, it is important to always be the one who reaches out, never keep tabs on whose turn it is to call – just pick up the phone, write the letter and let them know right now that you are thinking of them.

A while back my older sister came to visit us for a week. A few days in she laughed and said, "Grandma Elsie was gone before you knew her but by G-d, Nicole… you are just like her." My heart grew in that statement. I have always heard stories of my grandmother Elsie. She was born in 190-something, wore red lipstick, loved to host parties, had close friends she traveled with, and always danced until her heels came off (and then some more), and she gave to her community wherever she could. Sometimes in the form of feeding the homeless (in her home, y'all!) or driving the red cross bus.

These women knew the importance of having friends and being a part of a community. It is the life that my husband and I live in the hopes that our children watch us closely.

BEING PROGRESSIVE

Several of our non-child having friends have introduced us as, "that progressive couple who always allow children to any party they throw". I take it as a compliment because they keep rsvp'ing +1 to our events. Of course, I found a ton of research that supports children's development in having social outings that include kids with adults. Thank you, science, for making us not feel like bad parents!

Echo chamber or not, I think there are three components that equate to why it is good to throw parties in your home or bring your kids to one.

First, socialization comes naturally by interacting with multiple ages and seeing others model interactions. Second, there is massive frontal lobe development happening with how difficult it is for the brain to converse. They are seeing live and in action, the modeling of conversations between those who are more adroit at it and the difficulty those have who are not. The third and final component is responsible drinking. Kids who attend parties with their parents are seeing what people choose and do with alcohol.

They might still get mixed up in over imbibing, but for the most part, they will have a seed of knowledge planted that their parents gathered with friends sometimes there isn't any alcohol and sometimes there is. If and when their parents did drink it was as a social occasion.

Most importantly they will eventually see someone who chose to drink too much and pray to the porcelain gods. These living examples will do more to teach them than any proselytizing you choose to deliver.

PARTY FORMULAS

In math, there is an answer for everything. And as far as parties go there are three things to remember. First, people will eat and drink what you have for them. So, don't over buy - if anything you should have slightly less than you need. Second, you don't want to run out of food and drink early. Thirdly, always serve water. Guests should alternate water for every drink – more on how this will help abate hangovers and drinking in excess in chapter fifteen.

Using these formulas will help you reach a solid average for most events, depending on your collective guests' mood, and the time of day for your shindig, you might have a little more than you needed (hello, leftovers) or you will run out about an hour before people need to leave (and there's your cue for either pizza delivery or the door).

Estimating Drink Totals:
1 drink // per person // per hour // ex: 5-hour party X 20 guests = 100 drinks total

Estimating Bottle Amounts:
Wine bottle = 5 medium glasses
1-Sparkling bottle = 8 flute glasses
1-liter (33oz) soda bottle = 5.5 6oz servings
1- 750ml liquor bottle = (almost) 17 (1.5oz) shots

Estimating Appetizer Amounts:
5 servings per guest for first 2 hours //
3 servings per guest for second 2 hours

SUMMER PARTY PUNCHES & CELEBRATION EFFERVESCENTS

This page has been left blank for your planning or notes

This page has been left blank for your planning or notes

PUNCHY PINEAPPLE
Carrytail | Build | Jam Jars | 26 - 8 oz servings
Parenthood; when you vaguely mention something you all MAYBE MIGHT do some HYPOTHETICAL day and your kids take it as a blood oath.

INGREDIENTS
2 Large cans of pineapple juice (46 oz ea.)
3 Liters of Sprite
2 Cups Club Soda
6 Scoops vanilla ice cream

STEP 1
Combine pineapple juice, sprite, club soda in a large bowl (one that can handle 6.5 quarts). Chill before the party.

STEP 2
Add scoops of ice cream into your punch bowl just before serving for fun frothiness. Ladle into guests' cup and enjoy.

PUNCH & JUDY
Cocktail | Build | Jam Jars | 23-8 oz servings

Just when you think you might be feeling good about your mommy skills a trip to the store with your kids will put you right back in your place.

INGREDIENTS
60 oz. Vodka
60 oz. Pineapple juice
45 oz. Orange juice
10 oz. Cointreau
10 oz. Whiskey
0.5 Cup Honey
20 Dashes Peychaud's bitters
Slice an orange and lemon for garnish
Ice

STEP 1
Pour liquids into a bowl or pitcher (something that can handle 6 quarts) and layer in cut up fruit and stir. Put in the fridge to chill.

STEP 2
Fill your guests' glass with ice, garnish with an orange and lemon slice, and pour in your punch concoction. Enjoy!

SOIXANTE QUINZE
Cocktail | Shake | Flute Glass | 1 serving
People without Kids: "Sorry, I am late. Traffic was nuts."
People with Kids: "Sorry, I am late. My daughter's sweater was too sweater-y and the baby ate a band-aid."

INGREDIENTS
2 oz. Sparkling wine
0.5 oz. Lemon juice + peel for garnish
1 oz. Gin
1 tsp. Simple syrup *(see pg. 30 for directions)*
Ice
Fine strain

STEP 1
Combine lemon, gin, and syrup in a shaker with ice and shake vigorously for a count of 10.

STEP 2
Fine strain into a chilled glass, top off with sparkling wine, stir gently, and garnish with a lemon peel twist to enjoy.

GARDEN SANGRIA
Carrytail | Stir | Flute Glass | 2 servings

I think my favorite thing about parenthood is being spoken to in a patronizing tone by someone who needs me to tell her when to pee.

INGREDIENTS
Handful of leafy savory herbs (e.g., sage, thyme, basil, tarragon, etc) + extra sprigs
6 Cucumber slices + extra for garnish
2 Slices lime + extra for garnish
0.5 Cup Pineapple juice
6 oz Plain kombucha
Ice
Fine strainer

STEP 1
Take a handful of fresh herbs, 6 cucumber slices, and 2 lime slices. Muddle with the handle of wooden spoon. Fill shaker with ice and stir until cold.

STEP 2
Add pineapple juice and stir. Fine strain into your glasses. Top off with kombucha and stir again gently.

STEP 3
Garnish with herb sprigs (not thyme because the leaves are small and fall off easy… not a pretty picture for teeth!) Add a few thinly cut cucumber and lime slices to enjoy.

AUTUMN PARTY PUNCHES & CELEBRATION EFFERVESCENTS

This page has been left blank for your planning or notes

This page has been left blank for your planning or notes

ORANGE APPLE CIDER
Carrytail | Build | Punch Cups | 14-8 oz servings
Your mega-screaming-crying tantrum completely changed my mind. JK! No, it fu**ing didn't.

INGREDIENTS
6 Cups orange juice
2 Bottles sparkling apple cider
4 Cinnamon sticks
4 Whole star anise
4 Whole cloves
Candied ginger for garnish
Orange slices for garnish
Ice

STEP 1
Stick the cloves and anise into the orange slices then combine with orange juice in a punch bowl or pitcher (that can hold 3.5 quarts) and chill.

STEP 2
Just before the party begins pour apple cider into the punch bowl. Cut a slice of candied ginger halfway up the middle. Wedge slices onto each guests' cup.

STEP 3
Serve to guests over ice in their cups and enjoy.

BARRY HALL PUNCH
Cocktail | Build | Punch Cups | 13-8 oz servings
Raising kids is like a walk in the park. Jurassic Park.

INGREDIENTS
60 oz. Rum
20 oz. Apple juice
20 oz. Cranberry juice
10 oz. Elderflower liquor
0.25 Cup Honey
Slices of pink grapefruit

STEP 1
Pour into a punch bowl or pitcher (something that can handle 3 ½ quarts). Garnish with slices of pink grapefruit and stir. Keep in the refrigerator to chill.

STEP 2
Add ice to a guest's drink and ladle in the punch. Enjoy.

Don't want the punch to be watered down by putting ice in the punch bowl.

KENTUCKY FIZZ

Cocktail | Shake | Flute Glass | 1 serving

You never know how inappropriate song lyrics are until you hear your child singing them.

INGREDIENTS

1.5 oz. Bourbon
0.5 oz. Lemon juice
1 Tbsp. Raspberry preserves
Sparkling wine
Frozen raspberries for garnish
Ice

STEP 1

In a shaker add ice, lemon juice, bourbon, and raspberry jam. Shake vigorously for a count of 10.

STEP 2

Fine strain into a chilled glass and top off with a frozen raspberry to enjoy.

The fine straining will take longer than you want. This is because the raspberry preserves are thick and have seeds. Don't worry, it is well worth the wait.

AUTUMN BERRY BOUCH
Carrytail | Build | Flute Glass | 2 servings

Imagine the nastiest possible thing you could find on the floor right now. Wrong. It is already in my toddler's mouth.

INGREDIENTS
0.25 Cup sugar
0.25 Cup water
3 Slices fresh ginger
0.25 Cup Frozen berries or fresh
2 Cups Plain kombucha
Candied ginger
Ice

STEP 1
Make ginger syrup up to two weeks ahead with the sugar, water, and fresh ginger slices.

STEP 2
Fill 2 glasses with ice. Add berries and 4 tbsps. of ginger syrup. Muddle with handle of wooden spoon.

STEP 3
Top off with kombucha. Stir, garnish with candied ginger and a few berries and drizzle some of the ginger syrup over them. Enjoy.

WINTER PARTY PUNCHES & CELEBRATION EFFERVESCENTS

This page has been left blank for your planning or notes

This page has been left blank for your planning or notes

This page has been left blank for your planning or notes

WINTER PLUM PUNCH
Carrytail | Build | Punch Cups | 10-8 oz servings
Parenthood: wanting to be with your kid one minute and being tempted to sell them off the next.

INGREDIENTS
5 Cups water divided
Cranberries, lemon and orange slices
Fresh mint leaves
Cinnamon sticks crushed
1 Cup Plum jam
1 tsp. Ground cinnamon
0.5 tsp. Ground nutmeg
4 Cups Cranberry juice
1 Cup Orange juice
0.25 Cup Lemon juice
4 Cups Club soda

STEP 1
Lightly coat a bunt cake pan with cooking spray and add ½ cup water. Arrange the fruit, mint, cinnamon sticks in the pan of water. Freeze until solid. Add remaining water, arrange more fruit, mint, cinnamon sticks, freeze again. Let sit in the freezer until ready to use.

STEP 2
Melt jam in a pot until smooth, add ground cinnamon and nutmeg. Stir. Cool.

STEP 3
When you are ready to serve guests, pour in jam, spices, along with juices, and soda into a punch bowl (that can hold 3 quarts). Unmold ice ring by wrapping the bottom of the pan in a hot, damp dishcloth and invert onto a baking sheet. Place fruit side up in punch bowl. Divvy out the concoction amongst cups for guests to enjoy.

FEUERZANGENBOWLE (foy-air-tzahn-g'en-bow-leh ["g" as in goat])
Cocktail | Build | Teacups | 8-8oz servings
I always thought I'd be a patient parent. Then I watched my kid try to zip his own jacket.

INGREDIENTS
Enough whole cloves to insert into one whole orange, creating ascending lines down from end to end.
1 Lemon sliced
1 Bottle (25.5oz) Red wine (burgundy)
1 Bottle (25.5oz) Dry white wine
2 Cup Sugar
0.5 Cup Rum
1.75 Cups Dry sherry

STEP 1
Place all ingredients into a crockpot two to three hours before a party starts, set to warm. Stir occasionally.

STEP 2
When sugar is dissolved serve strained into a mug and enjoy.

Traditionally, the liquid is poured over a packed sugar log and set a flame before being ladled out to guests. Perfect for those cold German winters. I have modified this recipe assuming that you do not have access to a proper Feuerzangenbowle set.

SMOOTHBORE 125
Cocktail | Build | Flute Glass | 1 serving
Currently helping my son search for his chocolate ...that I ate last night.

INGREDIENTS
1 oz. Lemon juice
2 tsp. Sugar cube or 1 – 2 tsp honey (like clover)
2 oz. Cognac/Brandy
Sparkling wine
Orange peel for garnish

STEP 1
Build ingredients into a frosted glass, top with sparkling wine, garnish and enjoy!

CRANBUCHA
Carrytail | Stir | Flute Glass | 2 servings
My nickname is "Mom", but my full name is
"Mommommommommommommommommommommoooooooom"

INGREDIENTS
Four thin slices of fresh ginger
1 Sprig rosemary + extra
0.5 Cup Cranberry juice
1 – 12 oz. Bottle of plain kombucha
Fresh cranberries and an extra rosemary sprig for garnish

STEP 1
Fill two glasses with ice and set in freezer to chill. In a separate jar, muddle *(see pg. 30 for directions)* ginger and rosemary with handle of a wooden spoon.

STEP 2
Add cranberry juice and kombucha to your muddling jar. Stir gently.

STEP 3
Over a fine strainer, pour concoction into your frosted glasses. Garnish with a few cranberries and enjoy.

I recommend not using rosemary sprigs as garnish because the leaves tend to fall off the stem and end up on your guest's lips... no one wants that.

SPRING PARTY PUNCHES & CELEBRATION EFFERVESCENTS

This page has been left blank for your planning or notes

(This page has been left blank for your planning or notes)

SPRING BRUNCH PUNCH
Carrytail | Stir | Punch Cups | 14-8 oz servings
I cut the crust off my daughter's PB & J and I swear to G-d I hear her whisper that I am her b*tch now.

INGREDIENTS
59 oz. of Raspberry lemonade
34 oz. Ginger ale
24 oz. Club soda
Frozen or fresh Raspberries and mint leaves for garnish

STEP 1
Pour all ingredients into a bowl or pitcher (one that can handle almost 4 quarts). Chill before party.

STEP 2
Garnish drinks with frozen raspberries and crushed mint leaves and enjoy.

Frozen fruit helps to not water down the drink the way ice would.

FRONTIER PUNCH
Cocktail | Stir | Punch Cups | 11-8 oz servings

The best way to infuriate a parent is to open a second box of something when there is still a box of the same thing already open.

INGREDIENTS
1 Whole orange for peel and slices + more for cutting wedge garnish
1 Cup Sugar
1 Cup Lemon juice + peel from one lemon
1.5 Cups Pineapple juice
1 - 750 ml. Bottle Bourbon
1.5 Cups Sparkling wine
1 Cup Fresh or frozen pineapple chunks
Ice

STEP 1
Oleo-saccharum method: this is an old way of creating a subtle citrus perfume for cocktails, time-consuming – but worth it.
Using a vegetable peeler, remove the peel from one orange and lemon. Transfer to a large punch bowl (one that can handle 3 quarts) and add the sugar. Muddle *(see pg. 30 for directions)* to release the citrus oils, then let stand for 1 to 2 hours.

STEP 2
Leave the O-S from step one, add the lemon and pineapple juice with the bourbon, stir to combine. Slice the peeled orange add these slices and the pineapple chunks to your bowl, chill until ready for the party.

STEP 3
Just before serving add the sparkling wine to the punch bowl. Ladle into a glass with ice for each guest. Garnish with an orange wedge and enjoy.

FRENCH 77
Cocktail | Shake | Flute Glass | 1 serving
Some days it feels more like hostage negotiating with a bunch of drunken bi-polar pirates than actual parenting.

INGREDIENTS
0.5 oz. Germaine
1.5 oz. Gin
0.25 oz. Lemon juice + lemon peel
2 Dashes Orange bitters
Cherry for garnish
Sparkling wine
Ice

STEP 1
Shake Germaine, gin, and lemon juice with ice in your shaker.

STEP 2
Fine strain into a chilled glass and top off with sparkling wine and two dashes of orange bitters, stir gently. Garnish with lemon peel and a brandied cherry to enjoy.

BOUCHY SPRING
Carrytail | Stir | Flute Glass | 2 servings
And then I thought to myself, "What is the point of cleaning if my family is going to keep living here?"

INGREDIENTS
3 – 5 Mint leaves + sprig
3 Sliced strawberries
0.5 Cup orange juice + orange slice
6 oz. plain kombucha
Ice

STEP 1
Add the mint and strawberries into the shaker, muddle *(see pg. 30 for directions)* with handle of wooden spoon, add the orange juice. Then fill the 2 glasses full of ice.

STEP 2
Stir until cold. Fine stain into each glass evenly. Top off with kombucha evenly between the two glasses. Stir gently.

STEP 3
Garnish with an extra mint sprig and an orange slice or strawberry. Enjoy.

HOW OTHER PARENTS DO IT:

Eyes In The Back Of My Head.

"There is always a reason to have a block party here in NOLA. It is what we are good at doing. Our house is in the center of our block, and we have the longest driveway, so usually, parties are held at our place. The best I can do with four kids is try and pick up all the toys before people come over and clean the front bathroom because old people always like to get in out of the heat and I don't need nobody telling me I am falling down on the job. One time, I am stressing running around yelling at the kids to pick up after themselves before the party was going to get started and no sooner did I turn around than the baby took off to the front bathroom, I guess he thought he was helping me by cleaning the toilet. I come in seconds later and see him scrubbing the bowl with HIS TOOTHBRUSH! When he saw me looking at him crazy, he raised his hand out of the bowl and tried to pretend like he was going to brush his teeth. I juttered out NNNNNNNno baby that's nasty! Is there a surgery for getting eyes in the back of my head?!"

-Lynn - Mom of 5 crazy beautiful kids, New Orleans, LA

This page has been left
blank for your planning
or notes)

CHAPTER 15: HOW TO CURE THE HANGOVER

"Not all who wander are lost, some are moms in a store hiding from their children." -Momonymous

This is a very special chapter you are going to want to read closely about:

- Pre-gaming
- Infused waters
- Curing a hangover

For our last cocktail recipes, I give you a traditional Bloody Mary with her two sisters, Maria and Red Snapper, that can be gilded with some not so traditional garnishes.

Don't drink … … … in excess.

If you're thinking "Oh, okay, great. I give myself the same bloody advice every time I go out" – **look at the next page.**

Dr. Javid Abdelmoneim is an ER physician in the UK whose current life's work has been about educating the populace on health problems.

He used himself as a test subject through rigorous tests in the fascinating documentary, The Truth About Alcohol. He was attempting to find out what actually works in getting rid of the drunk feeling, and most importantly, abating the vengeful hangover.

What he found was that it all begins with three preparatory facets for our bodies. Developed muscle tone, drinking plenty of water before, during, after, and starting the evening with a full stomach.

WHY MUSCLE TONE?

The more muscle mass a person has the better their ability to process alcohol. This means that it helps in keeping you from being a one-drink-lightweight. There is nothing wrong with stopping at one drink, however, I'd like to not be drunk at one drink either. So, by keeping your muscle mass toned up you are taking preventative measures to keep from being the Sloppy Sally at the next party.

EAT ME, DRINK THIS

If you have a full stomach it makes it easier for the body to consume the alcohol. Specifically, protein and vitamin rich foods help metabolize the booze. If you hydrate with water before, during and after you are diluting the amount consumed which makes it easier to stay in the "enjoying myself" stage. Instead of rapidly progressing from, "this is such a pleasant evening, I am totally going to make this business deal!" to, "wow, when did the floor get so close?"

WATER WORKS

My think-they-are-so-funny-kids favorite quote to mimic me is, "Moooom, my head fell off!", "Oh, dear, have you had any water?" Well, Dr. Abdelmoneim definitely added fuel to my winning argument! Apparently, water should be the go-to for any ailment – especially diffusing alcohol. However, as much as I adore water, sometimes it needs a little pep.

Here are a few of my favorite water infusions to imbibe with:
- Cucumber
- Cucumber and mint
- Cucumber, orange slices, and basil
- Lemon slices and tarragon

First and foremost, when infusing water, everything should be fresh. Blood oranges are amazing, and baby or English cucumbers are my favorite. Word of caution, the piths of citrus (that pulpy white stuff) can turn the water bitter, so you may want to remove the fruit if you're keeping it longer than three hours in the container.

Any of the four concoctions listed above are easily made in a jar, pitcher, or large vessel. Slice up the fruit according to the amount of water you need. Typically, ½ baby cucumber, ½ an orange, 6 leaves for 2 cups water. Slap the leaves before tossing into the water to help aerate and release their oils. Add as much of it as you want according to your personal taste satisfaction. If you want more taste from something, add more of that. If you want less flavor, take some of the ingredients away.

HOW TO CURE A HANGOVER?

Scientifically, the only way to prevent a hangover is to not drink. Period. End of story.

But, our friend, Dr. Abdelmoneim needed to test this theory and all the wives' tales that go with it. He took three groups of people to survey with what might cure a hangover. He gave one group nothing …*that a**hole…*, a second group received ibuprofen, and the third had a fry-up, traditional English breakfast (i.e., beans, tomatoes, toast, sausage, and eggs).

After a rousing night of drinking to excess, the first group who would receive nothing, six out of six people had a hangover. Shocker.

The second group, the ibuprofen people had three out of six report relief from their hangover. In the final group, the ones who had a fry-up found that one out of six people found relief from theirs.

GRANNY'S ADVICE

My ole southern grandmother, Granny Nodine, would tell you in her gravelly-definitely-a-smoker voice, the only way to abate a splitting hangover is to have a "little hair of the dog" that bit you and go to work out on the farm. Personally, the stupid morning after, I want little to do with whatever I have indulged too much in; let alone work outside in blistering Texas heat.

However, I'll oft recover with a little of that dog hair …*who coined this, it's a gross idiom…* in these special Bloody M variations, take a couple ibuprofen, and go to sleep with a super dark and cold room.

WHY IT WORKS

We need the protein and vitamin rich foods to help metabolize our formerly lush selves. Celery, pickles, radishes, olives, tomatoes help replenish some of the vitamins lost. Tofu, shrimp, and bacon are chock full of protein.

There will be a little prep work beforehand for these special hangover cures but trust me… they are worth every tedious minute. Best time to do this prep work is to already have it on hand or cook it up before you head out for your big night on the town.

PILLS AND BAGS

Lately, the market has been flooded with "cure-all" pills that either flush your body with vitamins or enzymes to help your liver process and services are popping up all over with "banana bag" IV's and oxygen bars to abate the raging headaches and nausea. I mean, it is cool and all that I can take a few charcoal pills for the once in a while of being too stupid. I know I could have definitely used something like this while at University, ...*and also after that one night of falling into the kid's turtle tank...* but, maybe just less is more?

This page has been left
blank for your planning
or notes

BLOODY MARY
Cocktail | Tilt | Highball Glass | 1 serving

When I tell my kids, I'll do something in a minute, what I am really saying is, "Please be forgetful".

INGREDIENTS
3.5 oz. Tomato juice
2 oz. Vodka
2 Dashes Tabasco sauce
3 Dashes Worchester
0.5 oz. Olive juice
0.5 oz. Lemon juiced
3 Thin wheel slices of cucumber
2 Small basil leaves
Ice
For garnishes, see paragraph below

STEP 1
Rim half of your glass with a cut lemon and ground Himalayan salt. Place in freezer to frost whilst you mix your drink.

STEP 2
Put basil leaves and cucumber with lemon juice in your shaker and lightly muddle to release flavor. Add rest of ingredients with ice and tilt shaker back forth. Do not shake or stir.

STEP 3
Serve dirty, straight out of the shaker not changing the ice. Garnish traditionally with 3 olives and/or celery stalk that has been peeled to remove the strings from the back ribs and cut ½" lengthwise. Enjoy!

VARIATIONS:

Carrytail: if you are just wanting to have a vitamin rich drink, leave out the spirts.

Cocktails: *RED SNAPPER* uses gin instead of vodka following the same instructions. *BLOODY MARIA*, use tequila instead of vodka following the same instructions.

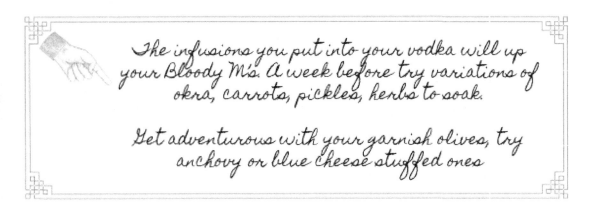

The infusions you put into your vodka will up your Bloody M's. A week before try variations of okra, carrots, pickles, herbs to soak.

Get adventurous with your garnish olives, try anchovy or blue cheese stuffed ones

A WORD ABOUT GARNISHES:

If you are not a vegan or vegetarian, I'd seriously suggest you try a good ole southern charm and fry up some chicken skin. The best way to do this is to remove the raw skin from chicken. Rub it down with cayenne, salt, and pepper. Then, fry it in peanut oil until golden brown. Set out on a paper towel to drain oil. Place in your mortar and pestle and ground down until a powder. This will keep for two to three weeks in the fridge. When you are ready to use, mix the powdered fried chicken with ground Himalayan salt. Then rim your glass with either honey or agave nectar, and dip into your fry/salt mixture. Place glass back into the freezer to harden up. Mix your cocktail and pour into your specially rimmed glass.

I love to also get a little theatrical with my garnishes and take a long toothpick and skewer various combinations of green olives, cocktail olives, gherkin pickles, little spicy peppers, pickled cauliflower, carrots, okra, and bell peppers. Then add some fried foods - tofu, shrimp, tomatoes to enjoy with my cocktail.

CHAPTER 16: A CLOSING OF SORTS

"Mom, I love you. You and Dad are pretty great people to be raised by. Thank you for always loving me through my messes."- My daughter aged 19.5

You have hung with me until the end and I thank you. Before I go, I want to tell you:

- Life and all its glory
- We are not alone
- Last words

For old time's sake, let's have one last drink, the infamous Mother's Ruin. This recipe was a formally kept secret of mine, it is a punch that is in high demand at our house storytelling parties. When friends and family were reading the final cut of this book and they found out it wasn't being included – there was a mini-revolt. So, to save my own life I have included it just for you – XXOO, me.

LIFE; AM I RIGHT?!

I heard a description of life the other day, and I cannot recall who or where it was from, but it wasn't the first time I had heard it described that way, so it doesn't really matter who said it; but what was said does matter.

"Life is not about getting from point A – birth, to point B – success, to point C – death. Like a symphony or a dance, all the stuff in the middle make up the essence of what it is" – paraphrased from the masses.

When you have to get up with the kids to make them breakfast, but you are consumed with exhaustion, the mother of all colds is attacking your immune system, and you are unaffordably late for work (again); that moment with them is the messy middle, the stuff from which life is made. Take a beat, take it all in, and remember all of it.

It is all too easy to set cruise control and pass each day until the next picture-worthy moment. That would be an egregious mistake that you will only recognize once it's all gone. Love this part too; don't wish it away and try to just get to the end. Love that you don't like it and that it sucks. It is the worst and that is okay; it is yours.

What I want to remind you, my reader, and myself, as I sit in the cacophony of my house trying to write this closing chapter with the worst cedar fever stuffing and itching up my face on the coldest day in Texas is that I can't wait until I feel good. Life is happening right now in these nanoseconds. This life right now is mine and I need to embrace the messy-no-good-horribleness as part of it.

If you can start to do that 1/20th of the time, then... just kidding - I am not a guru and I am not going to make any false promises or sell you some dogma. I just know the trying counts big time and we are better for doing that. So, try and see what happens.

WE ALL GO THROUGH IT

Throughout your life as a parent you will be fretting over all your decisions from, "Did I change their diapers enough? Did I play enough? Did I teach them how to work hard enough?", everything will seem to become the most important decision of your life. Yet, at the same time, everything will become unimportant. All the things before you had children that used to matter will cease to exist in your world or take a significant backseat to what matters to you now.

If I could offer you advice, it'd be to learn early on that it isn't your job to teach your child everything they need to know to become an adult. It is not your job to keep them from doing or experiencing "bad" things. Your job is to teach them how to navigate this life so that when they come across something they don't know; they know how to figure it out. When they get into trouble, they know who they can come to for advice on how to course correct. Parenting is foundational work. Make sure the basics are covered and the rest is being led by the hand of your child through their journey.

In this walk, you can have two children come from the same parents being raised in the same house and end up completely different from one another. You can meet two kids from totally different backgrounds being raised by two different parents who end up similar. Each person, be they small or grown, are on their own journey. Greek philosophers have taught us that contradictions represent a falsity. Eastern philosophers have been teaching us that both can coexist, and both can be correct. Parenting is full of hypocrisy and contradictions, that doesn't mean that you did it wrong or that you have no idea what you are doing. It is just what it is.

In the midst of your parenting, everything around you will feel like chaos. Most days you won't know which end is up, occasionally you will get to experience your child having a couple brushes with death …*always super fun*… and the next thing you realize, they are grown. Parenting as you knew it will be all over. Your heart will look back over memories and sink; tricking you to believe that you could have, should have controlled the chaos better.

It is a lie – don't believe it.

Chaos is often the mark of new beginnings. Think about when a revolution happens, things are thrown for a loop, but then structure and order arise from it. When a star is born in the cosmos, it is in a web of violence - then light emerges from the depths of darkness to reveal what has been created. To take this metaphor too far, when someone is cross-stitching a pattern, the underneath appears a muddy mix of chaotic lines, but when you take one look at the finished product from the other side it reveals conscious design choices and beauty. The mess is the work. Let it be messy. Learn to live in the swells of confusion and chaos; you are structuring a life.

Don't lose yourself in your fears. Stand up and look it in the face, breathe and walk forward in a choice you have made. Remember when we talked about iterations? You have the freedom as the author of your life and your parenting to choose differently when you need to.

During the writing of this closing my nephew, his wife, and two children came to live with us for a few months.

Their children are two and five. It has been a long time since I have had littles from day to nighttime-immemorial basis. We have had to have many talks of how our family does things, what our rules and expectations are… it takes a lot to merge two families together into one living arrangement.

This time with these young children, I am a different parent. I am an older mother with a wholly different vantage point, having to explain that from a place of teaching and communication has created reflection about my parenting, remembering when mine were that size. Questions of doubt and remorse crept in on how I never did enough, or I did it wrong.

I had to remind myself that I am not a prisoner to my past mistakes… they are there to show where I have come from. They are not there to shame me into remorse for a job not well done. They are there to say, this is what I have learned, and therefore I do things this way now.

My older two children met up with my husband and I for a family date. As the evening progressed, I sat back with tears in my eyes as they laughed and had moon and stars talks about big, BIG topics and I thought… "I really like these guys. They are pretty great people who still want to hang out with us and cuddle up to tell us their plans, dreams, fears for their futures." All of it was worth it. Every minute of each second was worthwhile.

I would do it all over again …*but I am so thankful I don't have to!*

Offering grace requires having grace for yourself. You are not always going to do or say it right. This is why there is a well-worn path to my children's rooms where I have gone in, hung my pride on a hook outside the door, admitted to them when I was wrong and asked for their forgiveness. Forgive yourself, Mom. Forgive yourself, Dad. You are doing the best you can with the skills you have. When you know better you will do better each and every time.

LAST WORDS

We all need friends. We need social time as parents. So often we can get stuck in our ruts, routines, and the downward spiral of our minds. Moms need other Moms, Dads need other Dads, parents need other parents to relate with, laugh with, and cry with - reach out and make those connections. Regardless of how long you are in a location find your tribe and care for it.

Don't minimize the impact that a good friend will have on your life and the rearing of your children.

If out of everything we were only able to teach three things to our kids and to ourselves - it would be, firstly, that we learn to do something to help ourselves first and foremost before we even ask for help from another. Secondly, to be equally brave enough to say what it is we want and need minus the passive aggressions or outright aggressions. Thirdly, learn to let it go and let it be if we can't achieve either or both one and two.

Be brave, cuddle your monkeys, make a friend, and forgive yourself. Then mix your favorite drink and tell me all about your journey.

MOTHER'S RUIN
Cocktail | Pitcher with Jam Jars | 8 servings
Here is to every mother who has eaten a candy bar in the closet because frankly, you just didn't want to share.

INGREDIENTS
½ Cup Sugar
¾ Cup Club soda/Sparkling water
1 ½ Cup Austin Reserve Gin
1 ½ Cup Grapefruit juice + 3 grapefruit wheel slices for garnish
¾ Cup Lemon juice
¾ Cup Red vermouth
2 ¼ Cup Chilled Champagne/Sparkling wine

STEP 1
In your pitcher mix sugar and soda water until dissolved.

STEP 2
Stir in gin, juices, and vermouth. Chill for at least one hour in the fridge.

STEP
Garnish the pitcher with grapefruit wheels. Pour in sparkling wine right when the party is getting started to enjoy a cup.

Mother's Ruin is apparently old British slang for gin. Perfectly named, right?!

This page has been left blank for your planning or notes)

AFTER PARTY

"If you have never been hated by your child, have you ever been a parent?" -Dadonymous

This little After Party has been included for you to easily locate key information that I have written about either within the covers of this book, additional information wherever you like to find it at library or the world wide web, and also me IRL.

- Cocktail Index By Spirit
- Carrytail Index
- Setting Up The Basic Bar
- Setting Up The Well-Stocked Bar
- Bibliography
- Where to find the author

To overcommunicate my too obvious disclaimer:

This book bares my soul – my mistakes and wins in parenting. Making me an expert not a professional. The drink recipes are listed at the end of each chapter because they are my favorite post parenting elixirs. Do not mix parenting and cocktails - that's what the carrytails are for! Decompress then imbibe with a cocktail. Enjoy this book, laugh and feel less alone in your journey.

Drinks by Spirits

BOURBON	GIN	RUM	TEQUILLA	VODKA	WHISK(E)Y
Fig Manhattan *pg. 182*	Cucumber Collins *pg. 127*	^Barry Hall Punch *pg. 219*	Ace of Spades *pg. 30*	Basil Martini *pg. 32*	^Glasgow Mule *pg. 69*
^Frontier Punch *pg. 232*	^Eastside Elder *pg. 55*	^Between the Sheets *pg. 193*	Agave 2 Ways *pg. 85*	Bloody Mary *pg. 243*	Golden Buddha variation *pg. 170*
Glazed Maple Old Fashioned + ^variations *pg. 201*	Emerald Spice *pg. 114*	^Cuban Reverie *pg. 168*	Bloody Maria *pg. 243*	^Fraise Martini *pg. 155*	^Irish Maid *pg. 99*
^Kentucky Fizz *pg. 220*	^French 77 *pg. 233*	^Feuerzangenbowle *pg. 226*	Daisy Verde *pg. 85*	^French Martini *pg. 155*	Irish Mule *pg. 68*
Kentucky Mule *pg. 68*	^House made Clover Club *pg. 52*	12-Mile Limit* *pg. 195*	^Distrito Federal *pg. 180*	^French Pear Martini *pg. 97*	Lavender Lemonade variation* *pg. 111*
Lavender Lemonade variation* *pg. 111*	^LaFleur *pg. 54*		Donkey Show *pg. 68*	Garden Mule *pg. 69*	^Medina River *pg. 111*
^The Manhattan *pg. 180*	^Lavender Bramble *pg. 112*		^Grapefruit Dazy *pg. 86*	^House made Clover Club variation* *pg. 52*	^Punch & Judy* *pg. 213*
^12-Mile Limit* *pg. 195*	Lavender Lemonade variation* *pg. 111*		^House made Clover Club variation* *pg. 52*	^Lavender Mule *pg. 69*	^Touchwood *pg. 142*
	London Mule *pg. 69*		^Lagarita *pg. 84*	Moscow Mule *pg. 67*	^12-Mile Limit* *pg. 195*
	^Mother's Ruin *pg. 249*		^Margarita *pg. 83*	^Punch & Judy* *pg. 213*	
	Primavera variation *pg. 129*		^Mexican Martini *pg. 124*	^Spicy Mule *pg. 68*	
	Red Snapper *pg. 243*		Parkside variation *pg. 185*	Sweet Kremlin *pg. 69*	
	^Soixante Quinze *pg. 214*		^Smog Cutter *pg. 157*	^3 Kids in a Cup* *pg. 109*	
	Southside *pg. 197*		^Spicy Rita *pg. 84*	Uzum Fizz variation *pg. 153*	
			^3 Kids in a Cup* *pg. 109*		

= referenced with other spirits
^ = requires other alcohol

Carrytail Index

Setting Up the Basic Bar

ALCOHOL
6 pack of beer
(go with a variety and pack your favorite, if you don't have one, the most liked beer across most taste palates is a pilsner or pale lager. My pro-tip is to try going with a small local brewer).
Bourbon
Gin
Rum
Tequila
Vodka *(kept in freezer)*
2 bottles of red wine
1 bottle of white wine

DIGESTIF
(a type of liqueur that was traditionally used in aiding digestion)
Orange liqueur

EQUIPMENT
Corkscrew/bottle opener
Cutting board
Elbow juicer
Fine strainer
Jam jar with tight fitting lid *(for shaking drinks)*
Knife
Large shot glass
Toothpicks
Wooden spoon

GLASSWARE
(minimum set for 4)
Jam jars
Rocks glasses
White wine glasses
Red wine glasses

MISCELLANEOUS
Angostura bitters
Lime juice
Ice

MIXERS
Sparkling water

PANTRY
Agave nectar
White sugar

Setting Up the Well-Stocked Bar

ALCOHOL
6 Pack dark beer
6 Pack light beer
Bourbon
Gin *(couple different types)*
Rum *(one dark, one light)*
Scotch
Tequila
Vodka
Whisk(e)y
6 bottles of red wine
3 bottles of white wine
2 Sparkling wines

APERITIFS
(liqueurs traditionally used to stimulate appetites before eating)
Cream de cassis
Dry sherry
Dry vermouth
Sweet vermouth

DIGESTIFS
(these liqueurs were traditionally used to aid in digestion)
Amaretto
Coffee liqueur
Cognac
Elderflower liqueur
Orange liqueur
Maraschino
Port

EQUIPMENT
Blender
Cocktail shaker with large-hole strainer
Corkscrew/bottle opener
Cutting board
Decanter
Elbow juicer
Fine Strainer
Frothier
Large fruit juicer
Liquid measures with smallest measurement of ½ tsp
Mixer
Mortar & pestle
Muddler

Paring Knife
Toothpicks
Vegetable peeler
Wooden spoon
Zester

GARNISHES

Brandied cherries
Candied ginger
Cocktail onions
Green olives
Pickled vegetables

GLASSWARE

(minimum set for 8)
Highball glasses
Martini glasses
Rocks glasses
Pint glasses *(heavy)*
Punch bowl with cups
Water pitcher
White wine glasses
Red wine glasses

MIXERS

Apple juice
Cranberry juice
Ginger ale
Ginger beer
Kombucha *(plain)*
Lemonade
Orange juice
Sparkling water
Sparkling cider
Strong coffee
Tomato juice

PANTRY

Agave nectar
Honey
Natural sugar cubes
Peppercorns
Preserves *(I like to keep a variety of berry types and fig)*
Salts *(have a variety of salts; at least a pink and white rock)*
White sugar

PERISHABLES

Bananas
Berries

Coconut cream
Cucumbers
Egg whites
Grapefruits
Heavy whipping cream
Lemons
Limes
Oranges
Tomatoes *(the small kind like a cherry or grape variety)*
Variety of fresh herbs

MISCELLANEOUS
Angostura, Peychaud's, Orange bitters
Ice & ice sphere molds

Bibliography

Chapter 1, An Introduction of Sorts

Carrie A. Nation (1846-1911), Crusader for Prohibition and for the Rights of Women - America Comes Alive. (2019). Retrieved from https://americacomesalive.com/2012/03/08/carrie-a-nation-1846-1911-crusader-for-prohibition-and-for-the-rights-of-women/

Carrie Nation. (2019). Retrieved from https://en.wikipedia.org/wiki/Carrie_Nation

Carry A. Nation - Historic Missourians - The State Historical Society of Missouri. (2019). Retrieved from https://shsmo.org/historicmissourians/name/n/nation/

Thomas, J. (1876). How to mix drinks, or, the bon-vivant's companion ... to which is added. New York: Dick & Fitzgerald.

Chapter 2, Obstreperous Age of Zero to the Truculent Twos

Afifi, T., Mota, N., Sareen, J., MacMillan, H. (2017) The relationships between harsh physical punishment and child maltreatment in childhood and intimate partner violence in adulthood. BMC Public Health, 17(493), doi: 10.1186/s12889-017-4359-8

Beebe, D., Rose, D., & Amin, R. (2010). Attention, Learning, and Arousal of Experimentally Sleep-restricted Adolescents in a Simulated Classroom. Journal Of Adolescent Health, 47(5). doi: 10.1016/j.jadohealth.2010.03.005

Bronson, P., & Merryman, A. (2011). NurtureShock: (p. Chapter Two). New York: Twelve.

Demos, K., Sweet, L., Hart, C., McCaffery, J., Williams, S., & Mailloux, K. et al. (2017). The Effects of Experimental Manipulation of Sleep Duration on Neural Response to Food Cues. Sleep, 40(11). doi: 10.1093/sleep/zsx125

Kruger, J., & Dunning, D. (1999). Unskilled and unaware of it: How difficulties in recognizing one's own incompetence lead to inflated self-assessments. Journal Of Personality And Social Psychology, 77(6), 1121-1134. doi: 10.1037/0022-3514.77.6.1121

Smith, B., (2012). The case against spanking: Physical discipline is slowly declining as some studies reveal lasting harms for children. American Psychological Association, 43(4). https://www.apa.org/monitor/2012/04/spanking

Straus, MA., Stewart, JH. (1999). Corporal punishment by American parents: national data on prevalence, chronicity, severity, and duration, in relation to child and family characteristics. Clin Child Fam Psychol Rev. 1999 Jun;2(2):55-70.

Vedantam, S. (2018). Baby Talk: Decoding The Secret Language Of Babies [Podcast].

Chapter 3, Terrific Threes and the Little Fu**er Fours

Adler MD, L., Bass MD, P., Turley BSN MSN RN, R. URMC/Encyclopedia/Urinary Incontinence (Enuresis) in Children. https://www.urmc.rochester.edu/encyclopedia/content.aspx?contenttypeid=90&contentid=P03083

Beebe, D., Rose, D., & Amin, R. (2010). Attention, Learning, and Arousal of Experimentally Sleep-restricted Adolescents in a Simulated Classroom. Journal Of Adolescent Health, 47(5). doi: 10.1016/j.jadohealth.2010.03.005

Benaroch MD, R. (2013). When a Child Can't Feel His Poops, conditions (kevinmd.com). https://www.kevinmd.com/blog/2013/06/child-feel-poops.html

Bronson, P., & Merryman, A. (2011). NurtureShock: (p. Chapter Two). New York: Twelve.

Bronson, P., & Merryman, A. (2011). NurtureShock (p. Chapter Four). New York: Twelve.

Demos, K., Sweet, L., Hart, C., McCaffery, J., Williams, S., & Mailloux, K. et al. (2017). The Effects of Experimental Manipulation of Sleep Duration on Neural Response to Food Cues. Sleep, 40(11). doi: 10.1093/sleep/zsx125

Escoto DO, M. (2018). Kids Health/For Teens/Bedwetting (Nocturnal Enuresis). https://kidshealth.org/en/teens/enuresis.html

Jana, L., & Shu, J. (2012). Food Fights. American Academy Of Pediatrics.

Melissa Halas-Liang MA, C. (2010). Top 10 Frozen Foods to Eat on a Hot Summer Day. Retrieved from https://melissashealthyliving.com/10-top-frozen-foods-to-eat-on-a-hot-summer-day/

Mayo Clinic, Patient Care & Health Information, Diseases & Conditions, Encopresis. https://www.mayoclinic.org/diseases-conditions/encopresis/symptoms-causes/syc-20354494

Talwar, v., & lee, k. (2008). Social and cognitive correlates of children's lying behavior. Child Development, 79(4), 866-881. doi: 10.1111/j.1467-8624.2008.01164.x

Tezuka, T. (2014). Takahara Tezuka The Best Kindergarten you've ever seen [Video]. Retrieved from https://www.ted.com/talks/takaharu_tezuka_the_best_kindergarten_you_ve_ever_seen?language=en

Tzu, S. (2018). The Art of War. La Vergne: Dreamscape Media.

Chapter 4, Friendly Fives and the Secretive Sixes

Baumeister, R., Vohs, K., Tice, D. (2007), The Strength Model of Self-Control, current Directions in Psychological Science, 16(351-355)

Bodrova, E., Leong, D. (1996) Tools of the Mind: The Vygotskian Approach to Early Childhood Education.

New York: Merril/Prentice Hall.

Laaser, M., & Laaser, D. (2008). The seven desires of every heart. Grand Rapids, Mich.: Zondervan.

Silk, D. (2016). Loving Our Kids On Purpose. Destiny Image Incorporate.

Chapter 5, Sociable Sevens and the Effusive Eights

Bronson, P., & Merryman, A. (2011). NurtureShock: (p. Chapter Seven). New York: Twelve.

Christakis, D. (2016). Rethinking Attention-Deficit/Hyperactivity Disorder. JAMA Pediatrics, 170(2), 109. doi: 10.1001/jamapediatrics.2015.3372

Galvan, A. (2010). Adolescent development of the reward system. Frontiers In Human Neuroscience. doi: 10.3389/neuro.09.006.2010

Tezuka, T. (2014). Takahara Tezuka The Best Kindergarten you've ever seen [Video]. Retrieved from https://www.ted.com/talks/takaharu_tezuka_the_best_kindergarten_you_ve_ever_seen?language=en

Chapter 6, Nucleating Nines and the Temerarious Tens

Gatto, J.T. (2000). Underground History of American Education. Odysseus Group.

Gopnik, A. (2016). The Gardener & The Carpenter. Farrar, Straus and Giroux.

Laaser, M., & Laaser, D. (2008). The seven desires of every heart. Grand Rapids, Mich.: Zondervan.

Silk, D. (2016). Loving Our Kids On Purpose. Destiny Image Incorporate.

Chapter 7, Edacious Elevens and the Tetchy Twelves

Bronson, P., & Merryman, A. (2011). NurtureShock: (p. Chapter Seven). New York: Twelve.

Galvan, A., Hare, T., Voss, H., Glover, G., Casey, B.J, Risk-Taking and the Adolescent Brain: Who Is at Risk? Developmental Science, (2007) vol. 10, no. 2, pp. F8-F14

Gopnik, A. (2016). The Gardener & The Carpenter. Farrar, Straus and Giroux.

Pink, D. (2009). Ted Talk: Motivation [Video]. Retrieved from https://www.ted.com/talks/dan_pink_on_motivation?language=en

Tibbits, M., Caldwell, L., Smith, E., & Wegner, L. (2009). The Relation between Profiles of Leisure Activity Participation and Substance Use Among South African Youth. World Leisure Journal, 51(3), 150-159. doi: 10.1080/04419057.2009.9728267

Chapter 8, Tenuous Thirteens and the Fragile Fourteens

Bronson, P., & Merryman, A. (2011). NurtureShock: (p. Chapter One). New York: Twelve.

Dweck, C. (1999). Praise Can Be Dangerous. Retrieved from https://www.aft.org/sites/default/files/periodicals/PraiseSpring99.pdf

Mueller, C., & Dweck, C. (1998). Praise for intelligence can undermine children's motivation and performance. Journal Of Personality And Social Psychology, 75(1), 33-52. doi: 10.1037/0022-3514.75.1.33

Ng, F., Pomerantz, E., & Lam, S. (2007). European American and Chinese parents' responses to children's success and failure: Implications for children's responses. Developmental Psychology, 43(5), 1239-1255. doi: 10.1037/0012-1649.43.5.1239

Chapter 9, Frightful Fifteens and the Scandalous Sixteens

Anderson, J. (2016). The Teenage Brain: Under Construction. American College Of Pediatricians.

Galvan, A. (2010). Adolescent development of the reward system. Frontiers In Human Neuroscience. doi: 10.3389/neuro.09.006.2010

Priolo, L. (1997). The Heart of Anger: Practical Help for the Prevention and Cure of Anger in Children. Merrick, NY: Calvary Press.

Strauch, B. (2007). The primal teen. New York: Anchor Books.

Chapter 10, The Sometimes Salacious Seventeens and the Edified Eighteens

Bronson, P., & Merryman, A. (2011). NurtureShock (p. Chapter Four). New York: Twelve.

David, S. (2017). The Gift and Power of Emotional Courage [Video]. Retrieved from https://www.ted.com/talks/susan_david_the_gift_and_power_of_emotional_courage/transcript?language=en

Levitt, S., & Dubner, S. (2014). Freakonomics (p. Chapter Five). New York: Morrow.

Talwar, v., & lee, k. (2008). Social and cognitive correlates of children's lying behavior. Child Development, 79(4), 866-881. doi: 10.1111/j.1467-8624.2008.01164.x

Chapter 11, Neophyte Nineteens and the Tolerant Twenties

Burnett, B., & Evans, D. (2019). Stanford Life Design Lab. Retrieved from http://lifedesignlab.stanford.edu/

Glucksberg, S. (1962). "The influence of strength of drive on functional fixedness and perceptual recognition". Journal of Experimental Psychology. 63: 36–41. doi:10.1037/h0044683. PMID 13899303.

Pink, D. (2009). Ted Talk: Motivation [Video]. Retrieved from https://www.ted.com/talks/dan_pink_on_motivation?language=en

Vedantam, S. (2017). You 2.0: Getting Unstuck [Podcast]

Chapter 12, Terrifying Twenty-ones

Kahneman, D. (2013). Thinking, fast and slow. Anchor Canada.

Robbins, M. (2011). Mel Robbins How to Stop Screwing Yourself Over [Video] Retrieved from https://www.ted.com/talks/mel_robbins_how_to_stop_screwing_yourself_over?language=en

Sinek, S. (2016). Simon Sinek answers The Millennial Question on Inside Quest with Tom Bilyeu [Video] Retrieved from https://www.youtube.com/watch?v=vudaAYx2IcE

Chapter 13, Paradoxical Times After 21

Barnwell, P. (2014) "My Students Don't Know How to Have a Conversation" Retrieved from https://www.theatlantic.com/education/archive/2014/04/my-students-dont-know-how-to-have-a-conversation/360993/

Covey, S.R. (2013). The Seven Habits of Highly Effective People. Simon & Schuster.

Editors of Encyclopedia Britannica. (2018), Prohibition, Encyclopedia Britannica, inc. Retrieved from https://www.britannica.com/event/Prohibition-United-States-history-1920-1933

Headlee, C. (2015) TedXCreative 10 Ways to Have a Better Conversation. Retrieved from https://www.ted.com/talks/celeste_headlee_10_ways_to_have_a_better_conversation?language=en

Pew Research, (2012), Communications Choices. https://www.pewinternet.org/2012/03/19/communication-choices/

Chapter 14, Jubilant Celebrations

Arjona, A., (2015), Why We Need to Expose Children to the Troubles of the World. Retrieved from http://www.takepart.com/article/2015/05/12/expose-kids-to-world-problems

Greenberg, J., Koole, S., Pyszczynski, T. (2004), Handbook of Experimental Existential Psychology. Guilford Press, NY, NY.

Singer, T., Seymour, B., O'Doherty, J., Kaube, H., Dolan, RJ., Frith, CD. (2004), Empathy for pain involves the affective but not sensory components of pain. Science 303(5661):1157-62

Chapter 15, How To Cure a Hangover

Abdelmoneim, J. (2016) The Truth About Alcohol. The United Kingdom. Sundog Pictures.

Chapter 16, A Closing of Sorts

Akta Lakota Museum and Cultural Museum, Four Lakota Values. http://aktalakota.stjo.org/site/News2?page=NewsArticle&id=8591
Arizona State University (2015) Who mothers mommy?: New research shows the critical role relationships have in keeping a mother happy, healthy and able to give of herself. Tempe, Ariz., https://www.eurekalert.org/pub_releases/2015-10/asu-wmm102915.php

Book Cover (front & back) Illustration Credits

Rocio Martin Osuna – all original artwork
***back cover inspired by https://www.clipart.email/">clipart.email</a>